SAN LUIS OBISPO COUNTY

JANET PENN FRANKS

CENTRAL COAST PRESS

San Luis Obispo, California

ISBN 1-930401-37-X

CENTRAL COAST PRESS
P.O. Box 3654
San Luis Obispo, California

Wineries featured in this book were chosen because they provided wine tasting without appointments, their locations were of particular interest to visitors, and they were in regular operation at press time. All winery photography is by Janet Penn Franks and Karl Wang (see page 159), except where noted. For more information about this book, see www.sanluisobispowineries.com. For more information about the author, see www.janetpennfranks.com. For information about Central Coast Press, see www.centralcoastbooks.com.

DEDICATION

This book is dedicated to my husband, John Franks, my personal, in-house wine guru, and to my friends Gere and Laura di Zerega, my winery book advisory team.

A special dedication goes to my sister, Laura Penn Harmon, in remembrance of our 2003 trip to "that other wine country," which inspired me to write this book.

Edna Ranch Vineyard, San Luis Obispo *(Photo by Janet Penn Franks)*

CONTENTS

ACKNOWLEDGMENTS

Individual thanks go to members of the San Luis Obispo County wine community, including Robin Baggett (owner, Tolosa Winery, and president, San Luis Obispo Vintners and Growers Association); Doug Beckett (owner, Peachy Canyon Winery); Bill and Nancy Greenough (owners, Saucelito Canyon Vineyard); Archie McLaren (founder and chairman, Central Coast Wine Classic); John Niven (director of sales and marketing, Baileyana Winery); Steve Rasmussen (winemaker, Talley Vineyards); Paul Sowerby (sales and marketing director, Adelaida Cellars); Brian Talley (owner, Talley Vineyards); and the many other San Luis Obispo- and Paso Robles-area vintners who took the time to share information with me about their wineries.

Special thanks go to Jean-Pierre Wolff (owner, Wolff Vineyards) for his time, knowledge, and support of this project.

I would also like to express my appreciation to those who helped in the preparation of this manuscript, including Ron Clarke, director of the San Luis Obispo County Museum and History Center, for giving me unlimited access to the museum's historical documents and photos; Gil and Dolores Babcock (owners, Eight Mile House), for sharing their historic home and vineyard with me; Giancarlo Bettinelli, for his knowledge of the wine industry; Gere and Laura di Zerega, for their ideas, enthusiasm, and support and for all the evenings we spent together enjoying local wine; Marlene Dube, for information about Tassajara Canyon; Nels and Vicki Hanson, for editorial support; Kirk Irwin, Samson Pinto, and Michael Urbanek, for their photos; Mike McMullin, for information about Tassajara Canyon; Betty Middlecamp, for her wonderful stories about her grandfather's life as a San Luis Obispo County vintner; Eleanore Weinstein and the members of the San Luis Obispo Historical Society History of Winemaking Research Committee, for their report; and Mark Wolff, for sharing his historic property with me.

And finally, special gratitude goes to my family: to my husband, John, for his enthusiasm, patience, the many dinners he brought home during the writing of this book, and his companionship on numerous weekend wine-tasting jaunts throughout the county; to my children, Allison and Erik, for their interest; and to my sister, Laura, for all her long-distance phone calls to follow the progress of this project.

FOREWORD

As aficionados of fine wines throughout the world are beginning to realize, San Luis Obispo County is one of the great wine regions. Its unique microclimates and soils are amenable to many of the most renowned varietal grapes, which are crafted into special wines by the area's highly proficient and dedicated vintners. To showcase these fine wines, some of the most comprehensive wine events in California are held here annually, including the World of Pinot Noir, the Hospice du Rhône, and the Central Coast Wine Classic.

To assist in the appreciation of the region's world-class wines, Janet Penn Franks has written a thorough yet concise guide that helps visitors to the San Luis Obispo, Arroyo Grande, Avila Beach, and Paso Robles viticultural areas efficiently seek out wineries in keeping with their interests. The array of wineries covered includes a majority of the fine-wine producers in the region.

Franks' book also gives the reader insight into the personalities that shaped the San Luis Obispo County wine industry, and profiles other individuals who continue to do so. In addition, Franks offers a variety of recipes provided by many local wineries to complement their featured wines.

Its combination of interesting and practical information makes this work a must-read for any visitor to San Luis Obispo County.

Archie McLaren
Founder and Chairman
Central Coast Wine Classic

THE HISTORY OF WINEMAKING
IN SAN LUIS OBISPO COUNTY

More than 100 years before San Luis Obispo County became internationally acclaimed for its fine wines, a local newspaper columnist predicted the area's imminent emergence as an important wine-producing area.

In the Oct. 3, 1889, edition of San Luis Obispo's *Daily Republic*, the writer declared that "soil and climate are of the greatest importance in winemaking, and the western slopes of the Santa Lucia Mountains are peculiarly adapted to the production of wine. The wine of this region will become famous in no distant day. We believe this because the wine made here is much superior to that of Napa, Sonoma or Los Angeles, the chief wine-growing regions of the state."

In 1889, no one knew how prophetic the columnist's prediction truly was.

San Luis Obispo County's winemaking history begins in the late 1700s, with the Franciscan padres sent by the king of Spain to colonize rugged Alta California. Spanish explorers in the 1500s had found several indigenous species of grapes on the Central Coast, but the native fruit was small, seedy, and sour, and unsuited for wine production. Padres at the newly founded missions in San Luis Obispo and San Miguel became the area's first growers of wine grapes when they planted *Vitis vinifera* vines, which were propagated from cuttings brought from Europe to California.

The modern-day development of the county's two world-renowned grape-growing regions—San Luis Obispo and Paso Robles—can be traced to these mission vineyards that produced wine for religious services.

SAN LUIS OBISPO-AREA VINEYARDS AND WINERIES

After Father Junipero Serra founded Mission San Luis Obispo de Tolosa in 1772, the mission padres planted a vineyard that would eventually encompass much of the city's present-day downtown district.

The region's ample sunshine, warm climate, and cool Pacific breezes provided favorable conditions for the cultivation of the mission's grapevines, which climbed on heavy stakes driven into the ground. The varietal became known as the "Mission grape"—early vintners described the fruit as "blue-black" and "round as a musket ball," and the vines as "abundant yielding" and "taller than a man."

The Mission grape yielded a sweet, harsh-tasting red wine that mellowed a bit when allowed to mature. Unfortunately, the grape's low level of tannic acid usually caused the wine to turn to vinegar before it could age sufficiently. Proper aging was also hindered by the absence of the white-oak barrels that the padres had used in Europe. Like European winemakers who produced brandy from poor-quality wine, the padres built stills and converted much of their wine into *aguardiente*, a 150-proof brandy. Mission San Luis Obispo soon acquired a reputation for the "ferocity" of its *aguardiente*.

It became customary to seal all local business transactions with a wine toast, a pleasant practice that lasted until the California missions became secularized in the 1830s and '40s and San Luis Obispo's vineyards fell into a state of neglect. Wine was no longer made in what would one day become one of the world's premier wine regions.

It wasn't until after the great drought of the early 1860s that area winemaking had a second birth. A Frenchman, Pierre Hypolite Dallidet, pioneered the secular commercial wine industry in San Luis Obispo. Oddly enough, the new, prosperous flowering of wine production was engendered by a European agricultural disaster.

In the 1870s, an epidemic of phylloxera—a root parasite that American vines were resistant to—ravaged the vineyards of France. Before the French could replant their vineyards with resistant rootstock, they needed to save their classic varietals. The French ministry of agriculture asked many French immigrants living in the Western Hemisphere to accept cuttings from the afflicted French vines and graft them onto hardy rootstock. In the early 1880s, Dallidet accepted thousands of cuttings, many of which were grafted onto rootstalk in his vineyard, which comprised nearly 10 acres to the south and west of his adobe.

The vineyard at Mission San Luis Obispo de Tolosa, late 1800s
(Photo courtesy San Luis Obispo County Museum and History Center)

With the help of his sons, Dallidet constructed a wood-frame winery adjacent to his adobe. The Dallidet winery produced high-quality wines, blending harsh, low-tannin Mission-grape pressings with high-tannin juice from European varietals. The Oct. 28, 1887, *Daily Republic* found Dallidet's wine to be "of excellent quality and the old wine of ten to eighteen years of age is considered by connoisseurs as the best in the world."

The owner of the first bonded still in the county, Dallidet also made brandy. The Dallidet winery, which ceased brandy production in 1890 and winemaking a few years later, no longer survives, but the original adobe home still stands at 1185 Pacific Street.

Dallidet and his grafted French-and-Mission vines had returned winemaking to the region. Now numerous vineyards were planted, and wineries were constructed beside the fields of growing vines. Winemaking began to spread beyond the mission city, to a nearby coastal valley where a failed marriage led to the creation of a local wine partnership.

South of San Luis Obispo, in the Arroyo Grande Valley, Englishman Henry Ditmas and his wife, Rosa, established Rancho Saucelito in 1880. Named for the many willow trees that bordered the property—*saucelito* is Spanish for "willow"—Rancho Saucelito's vineyards

The Dallidet family in their grape arbor, mid-1880s
(Photo courtesy San Luis Obispo County Museum and History Center)

were planted with Muscat and Zinfandel vines most likely imported from France and Spain. When husband and wife divorced in 1886, Henry moved to San Francisco, leaving Rosa and their young son, Cecil, to care for the vineyard. Several years later, Rosa married A. B. Hasbrouck, a Bostonian who owned the nearby St. Remy Ranch vineyard and winery. For several years, Hasbrouck's winery had made wine from St. Remy and Rancho Saucelito grapes.

Hasbrouck often advertised in the *Arroyo Grande Herald* that St. Remy sold "PURE WINES! Sweet Muscat, White, Riesling, Grenache, Dry Muscat, Zinfandel Wines, in any quantity—bottle, gallon, barrel."

A phylloxera infestation destroyed the St. Remy vineyard in 1915. A. B. Hasbrouck died the same year, but Rosa continued to make wine with Rancho Saucelito grapes at the St. Remy winery until just before Prohibition. During America's "dry years," Rosa Ditmas' family leased the Rancho Saucelito vineyard to several winemakers. (A number of San Luis Obispo County vintners ignored the Volstead Act that was in force from 1920 to 1933 outlawing the manufacture, sale, or transporting of alcoholic beverages in the United States.)

The Rancho Saucelito vineyard and homestead house, c. 1897
(Photo courtesy Bill and Nancy Greenough, Saucelito Canyon Vineyard)

In the early 1940s, the Ditmas vineyard and winery were abandoned. Bill and Nancy Greenough purchased the old Rancho Saucelito property in 1974, renaming it "Saucelito Canyon Vineyard." The Greenoughs restored part of the original 19th-century vineyard, bringing back to life the Ditmas family's winemaking legacy that thrives today.

San Luis Obispo's modern-day, commercial winemaking was born in 1968 in the Edna Valley, which lies on the southeast outskirts of the city. County farm advisor Jack Foote planted several premium wine-grape varieties, to determine if they would grow in the valley's calcareous, sandy-clay-loam and volcanic-rock soils. Foote's successful experiment became legendary and initiated the planting of the many vineyards that have earned Edna Valley a prominent place on the international winemaking scene.

In the 1970s, successful Southern California restaurateur Norman Gross established himself as a pioneer of the Edna Valley wine industry. On Orcutt Road, he founded Chamisal Vineyard, which is today the home of Domaine Alfred.

About the time Gross started Chamisal, the Jack Niven family planted nearby Paragon Vineyard. In 1980, Jack Niven (Paragon Vineyard Company) and winemaker Richard Graff (Chalone Wine Group) founded Edna Valley Vineyard. Several years later, Catharine Niven, Jack's wife, began Baileyana Winery. Former aerospace engineer Andy MacGregor planted his MacGregor Vineyard on Orcutt Road near the Nivens' vineyards, and, across the valley, Price Canyon Vineyard. In 1984, Margaret and Meo Zuech founded Piedra Creek Winery at MacGregor Vineyard. The winery and vineyard became Wolff Vineyards in 1999.

PASO ROBLES-AREA VINEYARDS AND WINERIES

In 1797, Father Fermin de Lasuen founded Mission San Miguel Archangel just north of what is today the city of Paso Robles. The San Miguel mission had two vineyards, one that extended east of the mission, and a larger field that lay to the northeast where Vineyard Canyon is today. Like the San Luis Obispo mission, San Miguel made wine for religious ceremonies.

About 12 miles south of the mission, one of the county's first secular vineyards was established before the American Civil War, and today the same land is still producing grapes for wine.

In 1856, Frenchman Adolph Siot and his wife, Paulina, arrived in the Paso Robles area and purchased land west of Templeton, where they planted Zinfandel grapes. Around 1890, Siot built a small winery and produced wine for nearly 20 years, until 1908 when he sold his wine operation to Joe Rotta. In the 1920s, Joe sold the business to his brother, Clement, who later bonded the winery after Prohibition and made his label well known for its hearty Zinfandel. The winery was sold in the 1970s, but after numerous legal battles it returned to the Rotta family. In 1990, Michael Giubbini, Joe Rotta's great-grandson, began replanting the vineyard largely to Zinfandel, the grapes Adolph and Paulina Siot had planted nearly 130 years before. In 2005, construction began to resurrect the old Rotta Winery building.

After the Siots' early field of Zinfandel vines, in the 1870s another family-owned vineyard was established to the south, in Santa Margarita, on the grounds of a lodging facility and dance hall built by brothers Edwin and Reuben Bean. The Beans' Eight Mile House provided overnight accommodations and refreshment for drovers and teamsters who traveled between San Luis Obispo and the Paso Robles area. The mild climate and the hotel's pleasant location and comfortable quarters made the inn a popular health resort for visitors from the Tulare Valley. Today, Gil and Delores Babcock own the historic property just east of Highway 101 and make wine for family and friends from the 280 Mission grapevines that still grow there.

To the west, across U. S. Highway 101, Tassajara Ranch owner Gustave Renkert first planted wine grapes in the 1880s, from cuttings he had brought from the Alsace region of France on the German border.

Renkert enjoyed a long career as a winemaker, and he continued to produce wine during Prohibition, as did several of the area's vintners. In January 1924, local authorities received a mysterious letter that described illegal activity "in the canyon."

When police raided the Tassajara Canyon homes of Renkert and two of his neighbors, many barrels of wine were discovered. At Renkert's house, officers found wine in the cellar, garage, barn, and in a nearby cave. The three winemaking friends

The vineyard at Eight Mile House, 2004   *(Photo by Janet Penn Franks)*

were charged with "unlawful possession of intoxicating liquors" and taken to jail. The next day, police confiscated all the illicit wine and placed it under a downtown San Luis Obispo garage for safekeeping. But in the end, Renkert and his neighbors avoided prosecution. The stored wine was left unguarded and later mysteriously "turned to water."

Commercial wine production in the Paso Robles area was often a family enterprise that spanned generations. In the hills west of Paso Robles, York Mountain Winery stands as one of the oldest continuously operating wineries in San Luis Obispo County. Owned by three generations of the York family, it was founded in 1882 as Ascension Winery by Andrew York, a native of Indiana who had come to California by ox team.

The Tassajara Canyon cave where Gustave Renkert hid bootleg wine, 2004   *(Photo by Janet Penn Franks)*

York purchased an existing apple orchard and a small vineyard that had been planted in 1874. Near his vineyard, York built his Ascension Winery, which he later renamed A. York & Sons. After Andrew's death, the winery became York Brothers Winery, and finally York Mountain Winery, when Max Goldman purchased it in 1970. Today, the Weyrich family, who also own Martin & Weyrich Winery, own York Mountain Winery.

In the second decade of the 20th century, Polish statesman and concert pianist Ignace Paderewski brought a wider public awareness of the Paso Robles viticulture area. A 1913 attack of rheumatism forced the virtuoso to cancel his California concert tour and retreat to the healing mineral waters at the well-known El Paso de Robles Springs. Enchanted with the countryside, Paderewski purchased 2,000 acres in the Adelaida area and named his property Rancho San Ignacio. Paderewski brought his grapes to the York family's winery to be made into wine.

Several families immigrated to Paso Robles and established vineyards and wineries in the 1920s—and at least two of these '20s-era family operations still flourish today:

In 1923, Frank and Caterina Pesenti planted a vineyard in Templeton with the guidance of their neighbor, winemaking veteran Adolph Siot. Bonded in 1934, Pesenti Winery was operated by

The historic York Mountain Winery, 2004   *(Photo by Janet Penn Franks)*

the Pesentis' grandson until 2000, when Turley Wine Cellars purchased the historic property and its 80-year-old Zinfandel vines.

In 1924, Sylvester and Caterina Dusi bought a vineyard east of Highway 101, in the valley between the Santa Lucia Range and the Cholame Hills. The Dusi Vineyard's old and coveted, head-pruned Zinfandel vines are still producing and are owned and cultivated by the Dusis' son, Benito, who sells his fruit to a few San Luis Obispo County wineries and to one in the Santa Cruz area.

In 1945, Benito's brother, Dante, planted another Zinfandel vineyard on the family property west of the highway. Today, Dante Dusi sells his fruit to local wineries.

The late 1960s and early 1970s introduced a new generation of winemakers and a modern wine industry to the Paso Robles region. Dr. Stanley Hoffman, a cardiologist from Beverly Hills, bought a 1,200-acre ranch northwest of Paso Robles, in the hills of Adelaida. With the help of legendary Russian-born enological scientist and viticulturist Andre Tchelistcheff, Hoffman planted the Hoffman Mountain Ranch. Owned today by Adelaida Cellars, the HMR acreage is home to some of the region's first Cabernet Sauvignon, Chardonnay, and Pinot Noir vines.

During the same period, several commercial wineries were established on the east side of Paso Robles, including the Rancho Dos Amigos Vineyard and Rancho Tierra Rejada. Estrella River, the largest of the "east-side" wineries, began in 1977 and is today Meridian Vineyards.

YESTERDAY, TODAY, AND TOMORROW

The mission padres' New World plots of the Mission grape were a prophecy of a unique grape-growing county whose vintages are now admired by knowledgeable wine lovers around the world.

By 2004, there were more than 34,000 acres of wine grapes in San Luis Obispo County and almost 128,000 tons of grapes crushed here a year. Local large-scale commercial vintners and small, family-owned winemaking operations are flourishing as the county's north and south wine-growing regions attract increasing national and international attention for their premium vintages. Numerous yearly wine festivals are hosted on the Central Coast to celebrate the production of an ever-increasing number of award-winning, world-class wines.

And yet the birth of San Luis Obispo County's modern wine industry harks back to the patient work of the first mission winemakers, as Old World knowledge and skill are grafted to new-age technology.

SAN LUIS OBISPO COUNTY
SUB-AVAs

RAGGED POINT

SAN MIGUEL

SHANDON

SAN SIMEON

PASO ROBLES

CAMBRIA

TEMPLETON

CRESTON

HARMONY

CAYUCOS

ATASCADERO

Paso Robles
York Mountain
Edna Valley
Arroyo Grande Valley

MORRO BAY

SANTA MARGARITA

LOS OSOS

SAN LUIS OBISPO

AVILA BEACH

SHELL BEACH

PISMO BEACH

ARROYO GRANDE

GROVER BEACH

OCEANO

NIPOMO

A FEW WORDS ABOUT AVAs

Location, location, location . . . .

It's as crucial in the wine industry as it is in real estate. Natural conditions specific to geography—sun, wind, rain, fog, elevation, and soil type—give every vineyard and the wine it produces unique characteristics.

Grape-growing areas with the same geographic conditions are referred to as "appellations of origin." However, in the United States "appellation" means something very different than it does in Europe.

In Europe, an appellation refers to a place name—Bordeaux, Burgundy, or Champagne, for example—*and* also describes a style of wine. European governments regulate which grape varieties may be planted in each appellation, and which cultivation methods and winemaking techniques may be used there. The purpose of European appellations is to ensure that every bottle of wine bottled under a particular appellation conforms to the authentic wine style of that region.

In the United States, appellations are referred to as American Viticulture Areas (AVAs). AVAs are designated by the Alcohol and Tobacco Tax and Trade Bureau (formerly the Bureau of Alcohol, Tobacco, and Firearms) as "official" grape-growing regions. Our government uses appellations to regulate *only* the geographic boundaries of the growing area—each winery within each AVA chooses the grape varieties it plants and its own manner of cultivation and winemaking.

The purpose of AVAs is to aid winemakers in distinguishing their products from wines made in other areas, and to help consumers better identify the wines they purchase. When an AVA is designated on a wine bottle's label, 85 percent of the wine must come from that AVA.

Currently, there are approximately 150 AVAs in the United States, but an AVA can contain smaller, sub-AVAs. California's Central Coast AVA, established in 1985, covers approximately 1 million acres and includes parts of Monterey, Santa Cruz, Santa Clara, Alameda, San Benito, Santa Barbara, and San Luis Obispo counties.

San Luis Obispo County has four sub-AVAs: Edna Valley, Arroyo Grande Valley, Paso Robles, and York Mountain. Edna Valley and Arroyo Grande Valley are located in the southern part of San Luis Obispo County, while Paso Robles and York Mountain lie in the northern county. These two distinctly different viticulture areas are separated by the Cuesta Grade.

"The Grade," as it is commonly known, is a descriptive term for the steep, mountainous stretch of U. S. Highway 101 that runs north of San Luis Obispo through a canyon of the Santa Lucia Mountains. Officially named "*La Cuesta*"—Spanish for "The Grade"—in the 1930s, the pass has a seven-percent grade that rises to an altitude of 1,522 feet above sea level.

The climate variation between the areas south and north of the Grade (or "below" and "above" the Grade, as locals refer to the two regions) is dramatic and greatly influences the wine styles of each area.

SOUTH OF THE GRADE:
SAN LUIS OBISPO-AREA WINERIES

The Edna Valley Sub-AVA

Established in 1982, the Edna Valley sub-AVA lies just south of San Luis Obispo and extends west toward the Pacific Ocean.

The Edna Valley sub-AVA encompasses nearly 29,000 acres of varied soil types, including sandy clay loam, volcanic rock, and ancient ocean subsoil. Many soils also contain calcium carbonate and/or limestone. Named for the small community of Edna that was founded in the early 1880s, the east/west-oriented valley is home to one of the area's oldest wineries, Edna Valley Vineyard.

The valley is bordered on the northeast by the Santa Lucia Mountains, on the southeast by low, hilly terrain, and on the southwest by the San Luis Range. The northwest border is crucial—15 miles from the Edna Valley, the adjacent Los Osos Valley passes through the barrier of coastal mountains and meets the Pacific Ocean. This gap serves as a wide funnel that sweeps cool marine air inland to the transverse Edna Valley, creating climatic conditions (and microclimates) that distinguish the valley from surrounding areas.

The Edna Valley enjoys long, dry summers with moderate temperatures. Frequent late afternoon fog that sometimes lingers until morning acts as a natural air conditioner, cooling the grapes after their daylong exposure to the warm sun. Summers are followed by short, cool, wet winters.

Often compared to the Burgundy and northern Rhône regions of France, the Edna Valley has a climate that provides optimum grape-growing conditions, particularly for the Chardonnay, Pinot Noir, and cool-climate Syrah grapes for which the valley is known.

Early morning fog lingers in the Edna Valley   *(Photo by Janet Penn Franks)*

The Arroyo Grande Valley Sub-AVA

Arroyo Grande is Spanish for "Big Creek." The Arroyo Grande Valley sub-AVA lies south of Edna Valley and was established in 1990. It encompasses nearly 39,000 acres of sloping land with mixed soil types, including calcareous marine sediment, sandy clay loam, clay, and sandstone.

The Arroyo Grande sub-AVA is bordered on the north by the Edna Valley, the Santa Lucia Range, and the south shore of Lopez Lake; on the south by Los Berros Canyon; on the east by the Los Padres National Forest; and on the west by the city of Arroyo Grande.

Like the Edna Valley, the Arroyo Grande Valley benefits from a diversity of microclimates and the coastal fog and Pacific breezes that moderate the temperature.

The coolest grape-growing microclimate is four miles from the Pacific Ocean, near the Laetitia Vineyard & Winery. Fog sweeps through the coastal vineyards, creating ideal conditions for cultivating Pinot Noir, Pinot Blanc, Chardonnay, and cool-climate Syrah.

Milder temperatures in the mid-valley area near Talley Vineyards are also favorable for growing Chardonnay, Pinot Noir, and cool-climate Syrah.

Optimal microclimates for Zinfandel and northern Rhône varietals are found above the fog line, near Lopez Lake and the century-old Saucelito Canyon Vineyard, where elevations reach 800 feet above sea level.

NORTH OF THE GRADE:
PASO ROBLES-AREA WINERIES

The Paso Robles Sub-AVA

Established in 1983, the Paso Robles sub-AVA is the largest in San Luis Obispo County, encompassing almost 610,000 acres.

Named for the city of Paso Robles, which in Spanish means "Pass of the Oaks," this sub-AVA is bordered on the north by Monterey and San Benito counties, on the south by the Cuesta Grade, on the east by Kings and Kern counties, and on the west by the Santa Lucia Mountains.

Paso Robles' geographical and climatic characteristics differ greatly from east to west:

The east side of Paso Robles lies on the floor of the Salinas Valley's southern end. Home to many large wineries, including Eberle, EOS, and Meridian, the flat plain comprises deep, black, fertile loam. Growing conditions resemble those in the Bordeaux and southern Rhône regions of France. Warm summer temperatures, skies without fog or clouds, and an absence of severe winds create an ideal environment for producing Petit Syrah, warm-climate Syrah, and the Cabernet Sauvignon for which Paso Robles is famous.

A cross section of limestone at Adelaida Cellars' Viking Vineyard
(Photo by Samson Pinto)

Paso Robles' west side consists of rolling hills that gradually rise in elevation to meet the range of mountains along the coast. The Pacific Ocean is less than 20 miles away and brings the west side of Paso Robles cooler days and nights and increased rainfall. The area's chalky, calcareous soils include weathered granite, serpentine, shale, loam, and clay. Like the northern Rhône region of France, the climate and mix of rocky soils allow westside vineyards like Adelaida, JUSTIN, Peachy Canyon, and Tablas Creek to grow many varietals, including Zinfandel, Cabernet Sauvignon, Cabernet Franc, and cool-climate Syrah.

The climate of the Paso Robles sub-AVA differs greatly from that of the Edna and Arroyo Grande valleys—temperatures on both the east and west sides of Paso Robles can fluctuate 50 degrees in one day. Most Paso Robles-area winemakers consider this drastic swing between heat and cooler weather the key to the varietal character of this region's wines.

The York Mountain Sub-AVA

The York Mountain sub-AVA is the smallest in San Luis Obispo County. Established in 1983 and covering approximately 6,000 acres, the area is tucked into the mountains between Paso Robles and Cambria and contains a single winery: York Mountain.

Geographic characteristics of the York Mountain area are markedly different from those in the Paso Robles sub-AVA—elevations rise to 1,800 feet, deep valleys crease the surrounding mountains, and a strong maritime influence dominates the weather. Temperatures are cooler, rainfall is greater, and soils are shallower than in east and west Paso Robles.

HOW TO READ A WINE LABEL

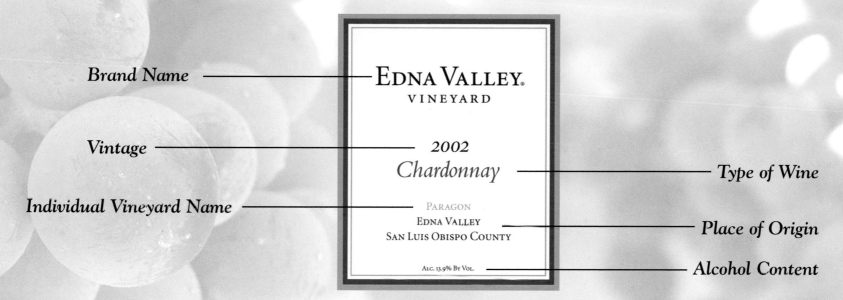

Brand Name — EDNA VALLEY® VINEYARD

Vintage — 2002 *Chardonnay* — **Type of Wine**

Individual Vineyard Name — PARAGON EDNA VALLEY SAN LUIS OBISPO COUNTY — **Place of Origin**

ALC. 13.9% BY VOL. — **Alcohol Content**

DEFINITION OF WINE TERMS

In the United States, the **brand name** or the name of the winery that made the wine is prominently displayed on the label.

The **vintage** is the year the grapes were harvested, not the year the wine was released. At least 95 percent of the wine in a bottle must come from grapes harvested in the year printed on the label.

The **individual vineyard name** usually indicates that the wine was made from grapes from an exceptional vineyard. At least 95 percent of a vineyard-designated wine must be made from the vineyard named on the label.

The **type of wine** usually indicates the grape variety or varieties used to make the wine.

The **place of origin** identifies the place where the grapes were grown, and does not necessarily denote where the wine was made. A state name—California, for example—indicates that 100 percent of the wine came from grapes grown within the state. An AVA or sub-AVA name means that at least 85 percent of the wine's grapes came from that specific appellation. A county name means that at least 75 percent of the wine's grapes were grown within the county.

The **alcohol content** is the percentage of alcohol in the wine, which usually ranges between 7 and 17 percent.

Other information sometimes found on the label is the description "**Estate bottled**," which means the winery owns and controls the vineyard where the grapes were grown.

"**Reserve**" wines are those deemed finer than the normal version of the winery's same wine.

The Alcohol and Tobacco Tax and Trade Bureau requires the **bottle's net contents** to be displayed in milliliters. Standard-size bottles are 750 ml and splits are 350 ml.

The bottle's **back label** displays information about the wine, which may include the vineyard in which the grapes were grown, winemaking techniques, and tips on food-pairing. Mandatory information includes the government warning by the surgeon general stating the health effects of alcohol (including impairment in operating machinery) and a "contains sulfites" warning if appropriate.

SAN LUIS OBISPO AREA WINERIES

SAN LUIS OBISPO
COASTAL
WINE TRAIL

ALAPAY CELLARS

CERRO CALIENTE

CLAIBORNE & CHURCHILL

DOMAINE ALFRED

EDNA VALLEY VINEYARD

KELSEY SEE CANYON VINEYARDS

KYNSI WINERY

LAETITIA VINEYARD

TALLEY VINEYARDS

TOLOSA WINERY

SAUCELITO CANYON

WINDEMERE

WOLFF VINEYARDS

"Wine of California...inimitable fragrance and soft fire...the wine is bottled poetry." —Robert Louis Stevenson (1850-1894)

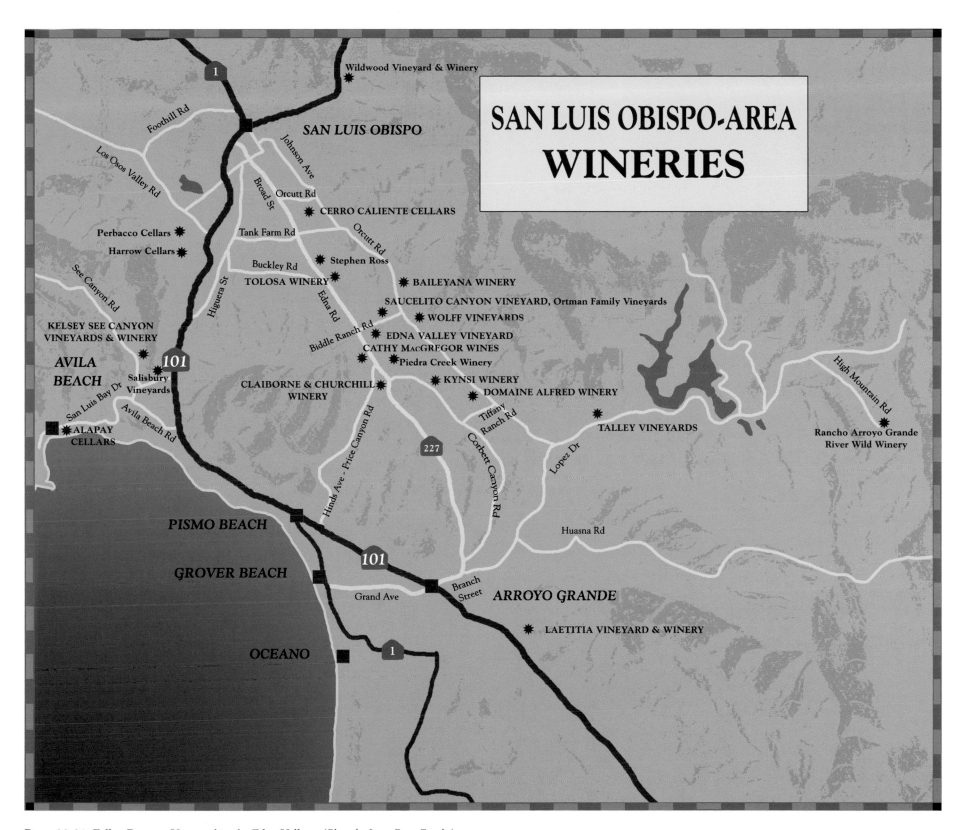

SAN LUIS OBISPO-AREA WINERIES

Wildwood Vineyard & Winery

SAN LUIS OBISPO

Foothill Rd

Johnson Ave

Los Osos Valley Rd

Broad St

Orcutt Rd

CERRO CALIENTE CELLARS

Perbacco Cellars

Tank Farm Rd

Orcutt Rd

Harrow Cellars

Buckley Rd

Stephen Ross

Higuera St

TOLOSA WINERY

BAILEYANA WINERY

See Canyon Rd

Edna Rd

SAUCELITO CANYON VINEYARD, Ortman Family Vineyards

WOLFF VINEYARDS

KELSEY SEE CANYON VINEYARDS & WINERY

Biddle Ranch Rd

EDNA VALLEY VINEYARD

CATHY MacGREGOR WINES

AVILA BEACH

Piedra Creek Winery

High Mountain Rd

Salisbury Vineyards

CLAIBORNE & CHURCHILL WINERY

KYNSI WINERY

San Luis Bay Dr

DOMAINE ALFRED WINERY

Tiffany Ranch Rd

TALLEY VINEYARDS

Avila Beach Rd

ALAPAY CELLARS

Rancho Arroyo Grande River Wild Winery

Hinds Ave - Price Canyon Rd

Corbett Canyon Rd

227

Lopez Dr

PISMO BEACH

Huasna Rd

GROVER BEACH

101

Grand Ave

Branch Street

ARROYO GRANDE

OCEANO

1

LAETITIA VINEYARD & WINERY

Pages 20-21: Fall at Paragon Vineyard in the Edna Valley (*Photo by Janet Penn Franks*)
Page 22: Horses, cattle, and century-old dairy barns create a peaceful landscape with vineyards in the Edna Valley. (*Photo by Janet Penn Franks*) *San Luis Obispo County Wineries* 23

ALAPAY CELLARS

Avila Beach's Alapay Cellars is as colorful as the town itself. The small, beachside winery offers a special wine-tasting experience with a smartly decorated tasting room, a fun-loving atmosphere, and 12 varietal wines made exclusively from grapes grown in California's Central Coast vineyards.

From the moment they walk through the door, visitors know they've discovered a different kind of tasting room—a whimsically painted mural behind the tasting bar reads, "Come on in, the water's wine." Proprietors Scott and Rebecca Remmenga believe wine tasting should be fun, not intimidating, and strive to make their guests feel welcome, comfortable, and relaxed. While enjoying Alapay's current releases, guests can lounge in chairs at the tasting bar, gaze at the 200-gallon saltwater aquarium of tropical fish, or browse the gift shop stocked with handmade items from around the world.

The first bonded winery in Avila Beach, Alapay Cellars was founded by Scott and Rebecca in 2002. The name "Alapay" is Chumash for "A World Above" or "Heavenly," words that the Remmengas feel accurately describe their well-loved beach-town community.

The small boutique winery produces limited amounts of each varietal—3,000 cases per year. Scott, the winemaker, explains, "Our measured approach lets us pay more attention to the great wine we're producing and give our customers superior treatment."

Alapay also produces several reserve wines, including the 2001 Bordeaux-style blend "Rebekah," which Scott made as a surprise first-wedding-anniversary gift for Rebecca (Scott felt the Hebrew spelling would lend elegance to the special wine). Scott's present to his wife proved to be a winner, as did other Alapay vintages: The 2004 San Francisco Chronicle Wine Competition awarded Rebekah a gold medal and Alapay's 2001 Reserve Great Oaks Syrah a bronze. In the 2003 San Francisco Chronicle Wine Competition, Alapay's 2001 Reserve Bien Nacido Pinot Noir won a gold medal, while its 2001 Viognier took the silver.

Alapay Cellars
491 First Street
Avila Beach, CA 93424
(805) 595-2632
info@alapaycellars.com
www.alapaycellars.com

AVA: Central Coast

Owners:
Scott and Rebecca Remmenga

Tasting Hours:
11 a.m. – 5:30 p.m. daily

Wines: Viognier, Chardonnay, Pinot Noir, Syrah, Zinfandel, Cabernet Sauvignon

Winemaker: Scott Remmenga

Southwestern Relish

1 11-oz. can Mexican-style corn
1 15-oz. can black beans, rinsed and drained
1 avocado, cut into 1-inch pieces
1 Tbsp. olive oil
3 Tbsp. lime juice
1 clove garlic, minced
2/3 c. red onion, chopped
1/4 c. fresh cilantro, chopped

Mix all ingredients together in a bowl. Cover and refrigerate at least 1 hour to blend flavors. Serve with **Alapay Cellars Viognier** or **Chardonnay**.

BAILEYANA WINERY

Described as "a woman not afraid to zig when others zagged," Catharine Niven founded Baileyana Winery in the 1980s on meticulous research, innovative thinking, and a hunch. Catharine and her husband, Jack Niven, pioneered the Edna Valley commercial wine industry and formed the Paragon Vineyard Company in the early 1970s.

While Jack grew grapes on a large scale, Catharine focused on her own project, a three-and-a-half-acre vineyard in their front yard. Despite what the grape-growing "experts" advised, Catharine followed her instincts, bucked the current growing trends, and employed the Old World planting style used in the Burgundy region of France. Making slight modifications to accommodate the differences between the Edna Valley and Burgundy, she remained convinced that the Burgundian approach would produce grapes of increased quality. Catharine was proved right—the grapes from her vineyard contained a tremendous concentration of varietal character. Soon Baileyana Winery was born.

Baileyana's tasting room is located in the historic Independence Schoolhouse, one of the few remaining one-room schools in San Luis Obispo County. Built in the early 1900s, it educated local elementary-school children until its close in 1956, when it became a private residence. In 1998, the old school was extensively renovated as a tasting room. Today, visitors can taste Baileyana's current releases and browse the fine selection of gourmet foods, specialty gifts, and apparel in the space where children once practiced the three R's. Beautifully landscaped grounds and a patio and picnic area beckon guests to enjoy the impressive views of the surrounding hills or play a leisurely game of croquet or bocci ball.

Baileyana's grapes are grown at Firepeak Vineyard, the Niven family's estate vineyard, which was established in the mid-1990s. Firepeak reflects 30 years of Niven viniculture experience and the family legacy of making award-winning wine.

French-born winemaker Christian Roguenant, a graduate in winemaking from the University of Dijon, brings his expertise to Baileyana Winery and Firepeak. Christian has made fine wines on five continents and has acted as a consultant to wineries around the globe.

Baileyana Winery
5828 Orcutt Road
San Luis Obispo, CA 93401
(805) 269-8200
info@baileyana.com
www.baileyana.com

Sub-AVA: Edna Valley

Owners: The Niven family

Tasting Hours:
10 a.m. – 5 p.m. daily

Wines: Chardonnay, Syrah, Pinot Noir, Sauvignon Blanc

Winemaker's Specialty: Pinot Noir

Winemaker: Christian Roguenant

Lobster Salad with Apricot-Walnut Vinaigrette

1- to 2-lb. live lobster
1 Tbsp. white wine vinegar
2-1/2 Tbsp. apricot nectar
1 Tbsp. walnut oil
1/8 tsp. white-wine Worcestershire sauce
1 tsp. dried tarragon
Kosher salt and ground black pepper
3 to 5 oz. mixed salad greens
8 to 12 cherry tomatoes for garnish

Place live lobster in a large pot of boiling water. Cover and boil for 7 to 8 minutes. Remove lobster with tongs, let drain in the sink, and place on a large plate. Refrigerate for 1 to 2 hours. In a small, non-metallic bowl, combine vinegar, apricot nectar, oil, Worcestershire sauce, and tarragon. Remove lobster from the refrigerator and re-move the claws. Open the body cavity and, with a spoon, remove the greenish-colored tomalley. Spoon 1-1/2 tsp. tomalley into the vinaigrette and whisk thoroughly. Season to taste with salt and pep-per. Remove all lobster meat from the tail and claws. Decoratively place greens and lobster meat on chilled salad plates. Garnish with cherry tomatoes. Drizzle dressing over lobster and greens and serve with **Baileyana Grand Firepeak Cuvée Chardonnay**.

CATHY MacGREGOR WINES & WINDEMERE WINERY

"My handcrafted wine is a journey that is rooted in the vineyard," says Windemere Winery owner Cathy MacGregor, whose viticulture heritage goes back more than 30 years.

Cathy's journey began in the early 1970s, when her father, local grape-growing pioneer Andy MacGregor, left his career in the aerospace industry for a new life as a viniculturist in the Edna Valley. In 1975, Andy planted Price Canyon Vineyard, and in 1977 the MacGregor Vineyard on Orcutt Road. Around the same time, he encouraged Cathy to pursue a career in viticulture and enology at the University of California, Davis, where she was already an undergraduate and would later earn a master's degree.

After UC Davis, Cathy honed her skills at several Napa and Sonoma wineries. Then, in 1985, she founded Windemere Winery in the Edna Valley, naming the winery after the MacGregor family's ancestral village in Scotland. One of the first female winemakers in San Luis Obispo County, Cathy made small amounts of her flagship California-style Windemere Chardonnay with grapes from Andy's Price Canyon Vineyard. "When your father is the vineyardist," Cathy points out, "you're assured the pick of the crop."

Cathy later created her second label, "Cathy MacGregor," which she considers her signature wine. Cathy MacGregor Chardonnay and Pinot Noir are made from the most select fruit of the Price Canyon Vineyard, the seedless "shot" grapes grown nearest to Price Canyon Road and the railroad tracks. The seedless fruit has produced award-winning Chardonnay vintages, wines that garnered gold medals at the 1992 California State Fair and the 1994 New World International Wine Competition.

But Cathy MacGregor Chardonnay isn't Cathy's only wine that has received top honors. Cathy MacGregor Zinfandel, made from grapes grown at the Benito Dusi Vineyard in Paso Robles, received a 91 score from *Wine Enthusiast* magazine in 1997. In 2000, Cathy's Zinfandel took the bronze medal at the Pacific Rim International Wine Competition.

Cathy also has a third, more economical label, her "San Luis Canyon" series. San Luis Canyon wine is barrel fermented with grapes from a variety of local vineyards, including Andy's renowned MacGregor Vineyard. San Luis Canyon features Chardonnay and Cabernet Sauvignon varietals.

Cathy MacGregor Wines & Windemere Winery
1600 Old Price Canyon Road
San Luis Obispo, CA 93401
(805) 542-0133
(877) 542-0133 toll free
cathy@windemerewinery.com
www.windemerewinery.com

Sub-AVA: Edna Valley

Owner: Cathy MacGregor

Tasting Hours:
11 a.m. – 4 p.m. daily

Wines: Chardonnay, Pinot Noir, Zinfandel, Cabernet Sauvignon, Merlot

Winemaker's Specialties: Reserve Cathy MacGregor Chardonnay, Pinot Noir

Winemaker: Cathy MacGregor

Shrimp Chowder

4 c. shrimp, shelled, cleaned, and deveined
1/4 lb. unsalted butter
1 c. red onion, diced
1 c. celery, diced
1 c. flour
4 c. <u>hot</u> chicken or shrimp stock
2 c. potatoes, cubed
1 qt. heavy cream
Salt and white pepper to taste

Melt butter and sauté onion and celery until soft. Add flour to make a roux and cook slightly. Add stock, one cup at a time, mixing well after each addition. Bring mixture to a boil, add potatoes, and cook until tender. Reduce heat, add shrimp and cream. Do not boil. Season with salt and pepper. Serve with **Cathy MacGregor Chardonnay**.

CERRO CALIENTE CELLARS

Don't let the size of Cerro Caliente Cellars fool you. This San Luis Obispo winery, which shares quarters with Don Peters Automotive, may be one of the smallest wineries in the county, but that hasn't prevented Cerro Caliente from creating award-winning vintages.

A four-time winner at the Indy International Wine Competition, the family-owned and -operated boutique winery produces small lots of "character-crafted wines for every taste," with grapes purchased from vineyards in San Luis Obispo, Paso Robles, and Santa Barbara County.

In 1990, Don Peters founded Cerro Caliente Cellars in the garage of his Paso Robles residence. Cerro Caliente—Spanish for "Hot Hills"—humorously refers to where his home was located and the scorching weather that usually prevailed at harvest time.

Peters moved Cerro Caliente Cellars to San Luis Obispo in 1998, to his automotive shop, where he built a temperature- and humidity-controlled wine storage room. Peters considers himself a *garagiste*—a French term that originated in Bordeaux and refers to vintners who make small amounts of high-quality wines in their home garages. Don often jokes that making wine in the cramped quarters of his shop is like working with a Rubik's cube—he must constantly maneuver pallet-sized "blocks" of wine bottles, grapes, barrel racks, and other wine-making equipment.

Following the current market trend, Cerro Caliente Cellars uses artisan winemaking techniques that gently process the fruit with minimal use of mechanical devices. Grapes are pressed with a hand-cranked press, and skins that float to the top of the fermentation vat are "punched" to the bottom with a wooden hand punch. Most wines are non-filtered and sulfites are added only when the wine goes to barrel.

Don says, "I spare no expense when it comes to making fruit-forward vintages with great aging potential."

Cerro Caliente Cellars
831-A Via Esteban
San Luis Obispo, CA 93401
(805) 544-2842
winecrafter98@aol.com
www.cerrocalientecellars.com

AVA: Central Coast

Owners: Don and Carol Peters

Tasting Hours:
Noon – 5 p.m. Friday – Sunday

Wines: Pinot Grigio, Chardonnay, Pinot Noir, Merlot, Cabernet Sauvignon, Cabernet Franc, White Cabernet, Syrah, Zinfandel, Multi-Viscosity blend

Winemaker's Specialties:
Red wines, blends

Winemaker: Don Peters

Carol's Cantaloupe Balls with Spiced Wine

1 c. Cerro Caliente Cabernet Franc
2 Tbsp. sugar
1 bay leaf
1 tsp. mustard seeds
1 tsp. peppercorns, crushed
2 ripe cantaloupes, chilled

Simmer wine, sugar, bay leaf, mustard seeds, and peppercorns in a large saucepan for 10 to 15 minutes, until slightly reduced. Remove from heat, cool, and remove bay leaf. Cut cantaloupes in half, discard seeds. Scoop out melon balls. About 1/2 hour before serving, spoon spiced wine over melon balls and toss. (Note: Spiced wine can be made one week ahead and stored in an airtight container in the refrigerator. Cantaloupe balls may also be served as a side dish.) Serve with **Cerro Caliente Cellars Cabernet Franc.**

CLAIBORNE & CHURCHILL WINERY

Among the many wineries of the Edna Valley, there is one that stands apart from the rest in its winemaking style. Claiborne & Churchill Winery has created an unrivaled and successful niche by specializing in dry versions of traditionally "soft-sweet" Riesling, Gewürztraminer, and other fruity wines.

Winery owners Claiborne "Clay" Thompson and Fredericka Churchill Thompson—former University of Michigan professors—left "the groves of academe" for the vineyards of the Edna Valley, where they founded Claiborne & Churchill in 1983. Their immediate focus was to create dinner-style wines with a harmonious balance of fruit, oak, structure, and texture, but they have since expanded their production to include Pinot Noir and small lots of dry-style Pinot Gris, Muscat, and an Edelzwicker.

"The wines are made 'dry' rather than 'sweet,'" Clay explains. "That's the key." He emphasizes that making dry wine is not a new but rather an old winemaking tradition long practiced in the Alsace region of France on the border of Germany.

Although two-thirds of Claiborne & Churchill's production consists of signature dry wines, the winery also makes small lots of Chardonnay, Syrah, Cabernet, and several dessert wines. Claiborne & Churchill vintages are handcrafted from grapes purchased primarily from vineyards in the cool maritime climates of the Edna Valley and Monterey County, and all are produced and bottled at the winery, whose architecture is as peerless as Claiborne & Churchill's distinctive dry wines.

The small, family-owned winery is housed in a "straw-bale" building, the first commercial structure of its kind built in California. The 16-inch-thick walls made of bales of rice straw insulate the building so effectively that there's no need for a mechanically operated heating or cooling system. The winery maintains a constant, "cave-like" temperature that is perfect for making and storing wine.

Claiborne & Churchill Winery
2649 Carpenter Canyon Road
San Luis Obispo, CA 93401
(805) 544-4066
info@claibornechurchill.com
www.claibornechurchill.com

Sub-AVA: Edna Valley

Owners:
Claiborne "Clay" Thompson,
Fredericka Churchill Thompson

Tasting Hours:
11 a.m. – 5 p.m. daily

Wines: Dry Riesling, Dry Gewürztraminer, Pinot Noir, Chardonnay, Syrah, Dry Muscat, Pinot Gris, dessert wines

Winemaker's Specialty:
Dry Gewürztraminer

Winemaker: Clay Thompson

Jambalaya

2 duck breasts
1/2 lb. raw shrimp, shelled and deveined
Salt and pepper to taste
1/2 lb. andouille or other spicy sausage, sliced
1 each chopped onion, bell pepper, jalapeño
2 stalks celery, chopped
1 clove garlic, chopped
3 scallions, chopped
2 c. chicken stock
1 bay leaf
1 Tbsp. each dried thyme and chopped parsley
Dash each cayenne and Tabasco
1 large can whole tomatoes, mashed with the back of a spoon
Hot cooked rice

Sprinkle duck with salt and pepper and roast at 350° for 45 minutes. Remove skin, cut meat into bite-size pieces, and set aside. Brown sausage in a Dutch oven and set aside. Sauté onion, peppers, celery, garlic, and scallions until soft. Add stock, bay leaf, thyme, cayenne, and parsley, and cook for a few minutes. Add tomatoes, duck, sausage, and simmer for 10 to 15 minutes. Add shrimp and cook until firm and pink. Serve over rice with Tabasco and **Claiborne & Churchill Dry Gewürztraminer**.

(Main photo and bottom right courtesy Domaine Alfred Winery)

DOMAINE ALFRED WINERY

"Ninety-five percent of what goes into the bottle begins in the field" is the winemaking philosophy at Domaine Alfred Winery in the Edna Valley. Terry Speizer, owner of Domaine Alfred, describes himself as "a farmer first" with an ambition to produce world-class wines by taking advantage of the valley's long, mild growing season and practicing Rudolph Steiner's principles of biodynamic farming, an innovative form of organic cultivation.

All Domaine Alfred wines are estate bottled from grapes grown at its Chamisal Vineyard, which was originally planted in 1972 as one of the first vineyards in the Edna Valley. Terry, a former Silicon Valley electronics entrepreneur, in 1994 purchased the then-dormant vineyard after the death of its owner and founder, Norman Gross.

Prior to replanting the vineyard, Terry prepared the soil in accordance with the latest viticulture findings from many prestigious universities—the University of California, Davis; South Australia University; and the University of Beaune in France, to name a few. Over the next four years, he planted clones of Pinot Noir, Chardonnay, four types of Syrah, clones of Grenache and Pinot Gris, and the original Chamisal clone of Chardonnay.

In 2000, winemaker Mike Sinor joined Domaine Alfred, bringing with him his own extensive knowledge, experience, and technical skills acquired from his many years as winemaker at Byron Winery in Santa Maria.

The same year, Domaine Alfred began the transition from conventional to organic farming—Terry and his team had become convinced that exceptional wine could be produced without chemicals and fertilizers. Today, Domaine Alfred is among the leading wineries of the Central Coast in organic vineyard farming, employing the

methods of biodynamics, a concept that brings "cosmic rhythms and life forces" to the process of grape cultivation. Terry is certain that these natural, innovative farming techniques produce healthy and exceptionally high-quality fruit and continually renew and reenergize the vineyard's soil.

Domaine Alfred continually strives to offer its customers exceptional wines. "If I put everything possible into producing exceptional grapes," Terry says, "then I'm half the way to making great wine."

Domaine Alfred Winery
7525 Orcutt Road
San Luis Obispo, CA 93401
(805) 541-WINE (541-9463)
tspeizer@domainealfred.com
www.domainealfred.com

Sub-AVA: Edna Valley

Owner: A. Terry Speizer

Tasting Hours:
10 a.m. – 5 p.m. daily

Wines: Pinot Noir, Chardonnay, Syrah, Grenache, Pinot Gris, Blush Syrah, Vin Gris, DA Red blend

Winemaker's Specialty: Pinot Noir

Winemaker: Mike Sinor

Chamisal Artichoke Dip

1 c. plus 2 Tbsp. Parmesan and Romano cheese (50-50 blend), grated
1 c. mayonnaise
1 8-oz. can artichokes packed in water (not marinated), drained and chopped
1 dash white pepper, ground

Fold together 1 c. cheese, mayonnaise, artichokes, and pepper. Place in an oiled crock, soufflé dish, or a thick-walled baking dish. Sprinkle with 2 Tbsp. cheese and place in 320° oven. Bake for 1 hour or until top is golden brown and bubbling. Enjoy warm with sliced bread and/or celery sticks. Serve with **Domaine Alfred Chardonnay**.
Recipe courtesy Nancy J. Stute, Domaine Alfred

EDNA VALLEY VINEYARD

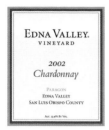

One of the Central Coast's pioneering wineries, Edna Valley Vineyard has been making award-winning wine since 1980. The winery is a partnership between Paragon Vineyard Company—the estate vineyard owned by the Jack Niven family and planted in the late 1970s—and Diageo Château and Estates.

Edna Valley Vineyard is located four miles from the Pacific Ocean, in the east/west-oriented Edna Valley bordered on the north and south by mountains. Evening coastal fog sweeps eastward though the valley, cooling the grapes that have ripened in the day's sun. This natural air conditioning allows the grapes to remain on the vine longer, mature more slowly, and retain sufficient acidity.

Of course, the land itself is of utmost importance in making award-winning wine. The valley's unusual layering of clay, volcanic rock, and ancient ocean subsoil helps grow the premium grapes that produce the winery's vintages. Edna Valley Vineyard's focus has always been its estate-grown Chardonnay, although recently Edna has made a commitment to producing Pinot Noir and Syrah with newly planted varietal clones.

At the Jack Niven Hospitality Center, guests can sample Edna Valley's wines—some varietals are sold only at the winery—and browse the gift shop while enjoying sweeping views of the surrounding Paragon Vineyards and the Seven Sisters, a line of dormant volcanic peaks. Guests can also experience the winemaking process "in action": year-round winery tours are designed to highlight specific, seasonal activities that are part of the sophisticated cycle of growing prize grapes and turning them into wine.

Edna Valley Vineyard has been the recipient of many awards. In November 2002, *Bon Appetit* magazine chose Edna Valley's Chardonnay as a favorite; *Wine Enthusiast* magazine recommends Edna Valley as one of the best places to be married in the wine country; and *New Times* rates Edna Valley's tasting room the "Best in San Luis Obispo."

Edna Valley Vineyard
2585 Biddle Ranch Road
San Luis Obispo, CA 93401
(805) 544-5855
hospitality@ednavalley.com
www.ednavalley.com

Sub-AVA: Edna Valley

Owners: The Partnership of Paragon Vineyards and Diageo Château and Estates

Tasting Hours:
10 a.m. – 5 p.m. daily

Wines: Chardonnay, Pinot Gris, Sauvignon Blanc, Pinot Noir, Syrah

Winemaker's Specialty: Chardonnay

Winemaker: Harry Hansen

Corn with Red Pepper Soup

1/2 c. olive oil
1-1/2 red peppers, diced (reserve 1/2 for garnish)
3 medium carrots, chopped
1 large onion, diced
2 ears fresh corn, cut from cob
1 qt. chicken stock
Salt and white pepper
2 16-oz. cans of corn with juice
Chopped parsley

Place oil, red pepper, carrots, and onion in a soup pot, cover, and sauté over low heat. Add one ear of corn kernels, chicken stock, and salt and pepper to taste, and cook until tender. Add canned corn and cook for 5 minutes. (Note: if soup is too thin, dilute 1 Tbsp. cornstarch in a small amount of water in a small bowl. Boil in microwave for a few seconds and add to soup.) In a separate pot, cook second ear of corn kernels until done and set aside to use as a garnish. Purée soup in blender, strain, and garnish with chopped parsley, cooked corn kernels, and remaining chopped red pepper. Serve with **Edna Valley Chardonnay**.

KELSEY SEE CANYON VINEYARDS & WINERY

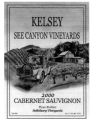

For most people, the mention of See Canyon in the mountains between San Luis Obispo and Avila Beach evokes images of crisp apples and mouth watering cider. But the proprietors of Kelsey See Canyon Vineyards & Winery, Dick and Delores Kelsey, want you to know that "apples aren't the only thing fermenting in the Avila Valley." The same soil that grows delicious apples is also producing several wine varietals.

The small, family-owned Kelsey See Canyon Vineyards & Winery is located one mile up picturesque See Canyon Road. The cool, maritime climate provides the perfect growing conditions for Dick and Delores' three-acre estate vineyard of Chardonnay and Pinot Noir grapes. Other Kelsey See Canyon varietals come from Creston, where the Kelseys' son, Richard, grows Merlot, Zinfandel, Syrah, and Cabernet Sauvignon on his own five-acre vineyard.

Since its founding in 1999, Kelsey See Canyon Vineyards & Winery has produced only small lots of each vintage "so the winery can focus on quality, not quantity," says Dick. Dick and Delores recommend that if their customers find a wine they like, "They should snatch it up," because Kelsey See Canyon wines sometimes sell out.

The Kelseys' wine is handcrafted by winemaker Harold Osborne. Before coming to Kelsey See Canyon, Harold was the first winemaker at the renowned Maison Deux winery in Arroyo Grande (today Laetitia Vineyard and Winery), where for four years in the 1980s he produced sparkling wine. He has a degree in enology and has made wine in Napa, Cambria, Santa Barbara County, Australia, and New Zealand.

At their "out-of-the-way" winery, Dick and Delores host a tasting room stocked with an assortment of wine accessories and glassware. Guests can sample an array of wines, including Kelsey See Canyon's signature Apple Chardonnay, a blend of 50 percent apple juice and 50 percent Chardonnay. The winery makes the distinctive wine as a tribute to the famous apples that have grown in the Avila Valley for more than 100 years. Kelsey See Canyon also offers sparkling wine, Zinfandel—the Kelseys call it their "monster" Zinfandel—and several dessert wines.

Kelsey See Canyon Vineyards & Winery
1947 See Canyon Road
San Luis Obispo, CA 93405
(805) 595-9700
info@kelseywine.com
www.kelseywine.com

AVA: Central Coast

Owners: Dick, Delores, Richard, and Keith Kelsey

Tasting Hours:
Noon – 5:30 p.m. daily

Wines: Cabernet Sauvignon, Merlot, Zinfandel, Pinot Noir, Syrah, Chardonnay, White Zinfandel, Apple Chardonnay, dessert wines, sparkling wines

Winemaker's Specialty: Sparkling wines

Winemaker: Harold Osborne

Mushroom Parmesan Crostini

1 Tbsp. olive oil
1 clove garlic, finely chopped
1 c. mushrooms, chopped
1 12-inch-long loaf Italian or French bread, cut into 12 slices and toasted
3/4 c. prepared pizza sauce
1/4 c. Parmesan cheese, grated
1 Tbsp. fresh basil leaves, chopped, or 1 tsp. dried basil

In an 8-inch non-stick skillet, sauté garlic in oil for 30 seconds. Add mushrooms and cook, occasionally stirring, for 2 minutes or until liquid evaporates. Arrange bread slices on a baking sheet, spread with pizza sauce, and top with mushroom mixture, cheese, and basil. Bake at 375° for 15 minutes or until heated through. Serve with **Kelsey See Canyon Pinot Noir**.

KYNSI WINERY

On the historic Rancho Corral de Piedra in the heart of the Edna Valley, an agricultural past and modern state-of-the-art technology coexist within the walls of a converted 1940s dairy barn. Where dairymen once milked cows at morning and evening, Kynsi Winery now employs a high-tech wine-transferring method using an innovative tool called the "Bulldog Pup," a successful and popular creation invented by one-half of Kynsi's husband-and-wife winemaking team.

Don and Gwen Othman founded the small, family-owned Kynsi Winery in 1995 to produce high-quality, single-vineyard wines from grapes of select Central Coast vineyards. Gwen says, "Kynsi's concern for quality from vineyard to bottle is evident in our elegant, lush, generously complex wines that embody distinctive *terroir* and varietal characteristics."

In 2002, the Othmans received official acclaim for their winemaking labors—their 1999 Syrah was awarded "Best Syrah of California" in the California State Fair Commercial Wine Competition. Don and Gwen's further quest for excellent wines produced from premium grapes led them to plant Stone Corral, their estate Pinot Noir vineyard.

The Othmans' winemaking success was sweet, although a decade before the advent of their Kynsi Winery the Othmans had already made a dramatic impact on the world of fine wines. In 1986, Don invented the Bulldog Pup, a gas-pressurized, wine-racking tool that revolutionized wine-transferring methods in wine cellars all over the world. The Bulldog Pup delivers nitrogen gas into the top of the barrel—or other vessel—creating gas pressure that gently pushes the wine out the transfer hose. The wine is not pumped, agitated, or exposed to oxygen, thus protecting its delicate varietal character and color, which is especially important in producing fragile Pinot Noir and white wines.

The Kynsi tasting room is located in the old dairy barn's milk-processing room where the original cold-room door leads to the wine vault. Under high, coved ceilings, visitors can taste Kynsi's fine selection of current releases while soaking up the cozy ambience of a bygone era of Central Coast farm life.

"Kynsi"—meaning "Talon" in Finnish (the Othmans' ancestry)—is a reference to resident barn owls that play a vital role at the winery by naturally controlling gophers in the vineyard and gardens. In a tribute to these fascinating birds of prey, a picture of a barn owl appears on the Kynsi label.

Kynsi Winery
2212 Corbett Canyon Road
Arroyo Grande, CA 93420
(805) 544-8461
info@kynsi.com
www.kynsi.com

Sub-AVA: Edna Valley

Owners: Don and Gwen Othman

Tasting Hours:
11 a.m. – 5 p.m. Thurs. – Mon. (Summer)
11 a.m. – 5 p.m. Fri. – Sun. (Winter)

Wines: Chardonnay, Pinot Noir, Syrah, Merrah, Zinfandel, Pinot Blanc

Winemakers' Specialty: Stone Corral Vineyard Estate Pinot Noir

Winemakers:
Don and Gwen Othman

Crab and White Corn Chowder

10 oz. lump crab meat, cooked
4 c. chicken or shellfish stock
3 c. white petite corn, fresh or frozen
2 Tbsp. olive oil
1 tsp. ginger, finely chopped
1-1/2 c. onion, diced
1/2 c. celery, diced
1/4 c. red bell pepper, minced
1/4 tsp. chopped chipotle chili in adobo sauce
2 to 3 c. waxy potatoes, peeled and diced
1 c. Kynsi Pinot Blanc.

3/4 c. cream, heavy or light
1/3 c. fresh cilantro, chopped (optional)
Kosher salt and freshly ground black pepper

In a stockpot, sauté ginger in olive oil until soft. Add onions, celery, red pepper, and chipotle, and sauté over medium heat for 2 minutes. Add potatoes, wine, and stock, and bring to a boil. Reduce heat and simmer about 8 minutes until potatoes are almost done. In a blender, combine 1 cup of the corn with 1 cup of the hot stock and blend until smooth. Return mixture to stockpot and add remaining corn kernels, cream, and crab meat. Warm until just heated through and season to taste with salt and pepper. Stir in cilantro just before serving if desired. Serve with **Kynsi Pinot Blanc**.

LAETITIA VINEYARD & WINERY

"Winemaking is a business for tortoises, not hares," says Laetitia Vineyard & Winery owner Selim Zilkha, who believes in "growing the business bottle by bottle." Selim's philosophy of extreme patience and care has paid off richly—Laetitia has received numerous awards for its world-class Burgundian wines.

Laetitia's beginnings can be traced to the inspired insight of French viticulturists from the esteemed champagne house Champagne Deutz. In 1982, they were searching California for a suitable area to plant a vineyard for Méthode Champenoise sparkling wines. The Arroyo Grande Valley, located four miles from the ocean, offered a temperate, marine climate and rich volcanic soil that reminded the French grape growers of their native Epernay. They also found the topography of the valley desirable, with its multitude of rolling hills that ensured good drainage. Soon, Maison Deutz was born.

In the ensuing years, the winery changed hands twice and was renamed "Laetitia" after one of the owner's daughters. In 1998, the 185-acre vineyard was bought by a partnership that included Selim Zilkha. Selim and his partners planted 415 acres of Pinot Noir, Pinot Blanc, and Chardonnay grapes and several acres of Syrah, which went in on the warmer, easternmost section of the property.

Today, Laetitia Vineyard & Winery maintains a serious commitment to making its award-winning Pinot Noir. Also known for Pinot Blanc, Chardonnay, Syrah, and small quantities of Méthode Champenoise sparkling wine, "Laetitia produces wines that exhibit delicious fruit flavors, true varietal characteristics, excellent color, and bright acidity," says Selim.

The quality of Laetitia's wines is evident from the many awards it has received: Laetitia's vintages have taken top honors at the San Francisco Chronicle Wine Competition, the Florida State Fair International Wine & Grape Juice Competition, and the Los Angeles County Fair Wine Competition, and have been recommended by many wine publications, including *Connoisseur's Guide to California Wine* and *Wine Enthusiast*.

But award-winning wine isn't the only reason to visit Laetitia Vineyard & Winery. Laetitia's hilltop visitor center, gift shop, and picnic area offer guests commanding views of the vineyards, the Arroyo Grande Valley, and the Pacific Ocean.

Laetitia Vineyard & Winery
453 Laetitia Vineyard Drive
Arroyo Grande, CA 93420
(805) 481-1772
info@laetitiawine.com
www.laetitiawine.com

Sub-AVA: Arroyo Grande Valley

Owner: Selim Zilkha

Tasting Hours:
11 a.m. – 5 p.m. daily

Wines: Pinot Noir, Pinot Blanc, Chardonnay, Syrah, sparkling wine

Winemaker's Specialty:
Pinot Noir

Winemaker: Eric Hickey

Grilled Dijon-Basil Salmon

4 salmon fillets (6 to 8 oz. each)
1/4 c. extra-virgin olive oil
1 Tbsp. fresh basil, finely chopped
2 cloves garlic, finely diced
Freshly ground pepper
Maldon's salt flakes (or coarse kosher salt)
1 tsp. fresh lemon juice
1 tsp. Dijon mustard
1/4 c. Laetitia Estate Pinot Noir

Mix olive oil, basil, garlic, pepper, lemon, and Pinot Noir in a bowl and set aside. Remove skin from fish, if desired, and baste salmon on both sides with marinade. Lightly sprinkle fish with salt flakes. Place fish on a hot charcoal grill for about 3 to 4 minutes per side. Fish can also be prepared in a hot sauté pan. Serve with **Laetitia Estate Pinot Noir**.

(Photos courtesy Laetitia Vineyard & Winery)

SAUCELITO CANYON VINEYARD

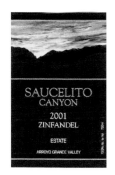

Saucelito Canyon Vineyard is one of San Luis Obispo County's oldest vineyards, dating back to 1880 when Englishman Henry Ditmas and his wife, Rosa, planted several acres of Muscat and Zinfandel vines. The Ditmas vineyard was called "Rancho Saucelito" and remained in the family for three generations, until 1974, when Bill and Nancy Greenough purchased the property from the Ditmases' granddaughters.

Bill painstakingly restored three acres of the original 19th-century vineyard, which had lain abandoned since World War II. He removed dead debris from the root crowns and pruned the shoots, leaving the strongest to grow and form new trunks. Today, the resulting dry-farmed Zinfandel vines provide the foundation for Saucelito Canyon Vineyard's award-winning estate wine.

After resurrecting Henry Ditmas' 1880s-era vines, Bill took cuttings to plant a new Zinfandel vineyard as well as three acres of Bordeaux varieties—Cabernet Sauvignon, Merlot, Cabernet Franc, and Malbec. Bill gave cuttings to the University of California, Davis, where they became part of its Heritage Vineyard, an unusual and unprecedented collection of rare and "famous" Zinfandel vine cuttings from all over California.

The Saucelito Canyon tasting room makes its home in the Edna Valley, while the historic Ditmas vineyard lies in the nearby Arroyo Grande Valley, where surrounding mountain ridges moderate the influx of cool, coastal air. Bill explains that Saucelito remains cooler than most Zinfandel vineyards and produces "elegant, full-bodied, nicely balanced Zinfandel wine" different from most Zinfandels, "which are one-dimensional, kind of like a big fruit bomb."

Bill believes there's a big advantage in having his vineyard so close to his winery: Every bin of grapes can be checked as it's picked. "Zinfandel is typically hard to sample because not all parts of the grape cluster ripen at the same time," Bill points out. "If a bin comes in that isn't ready to be processed, the pickers move to another location in the vineyard."

Saucelito Canyon Vineyard
3080 Biddle Ranch Road
San Luis Obispo, CA 93401
(805) 543-2111
info@saucelitocanyon.com
www.saucelitocanyon.com

Sub-AVA: Arroyo Grande Valley

Owners:
Bill and Nancy Greenough

Tasting Hours:
10 a.m. – 5 p.m. Thursday – Monday

Wines: Zinfandel, Cabernet Sauvignon

Winemaker's Specialty: Zinfandel

Winemaker: Bill Greenough

Raspberry Pork Chops

1 Tbsp. butter
1 Tbsp. olive oil
3 lbs. pork loin chops or roast
1/2 c. raspberry vinegar, divided
3 cloves garlic, thinly sliced
2 tomatoes, seeded and chopped
1 tsp. dried thyme
1 Tbsp. each, freshly chopped parsley and sage
1/2 c. chicken stock
Salt and pepper to taste
Fresh raspberries for garnish

Melt butter in skillet, add oil, and brown meat on each side. Pour off fat, reduce heat to medium low, and add garlic and 2 Tbsp. vinegar. Cover. Simmer for 10 minutes. Remove pork to heated plate and keep warm. Add remaining vinegar to pan, stirring up brown bits from bottom. Raise heat and boil until vinegar is reduced to a thick glaze. Add tomatoes, parsley, sage, and chicken stock. Boil until liquid is reduced to half and strain. Season with salt and pepper. Spoon sauce over pork, and garnish with berries and thyme. Serve with **Saucelito Canyon Zinfandel**.

TALLEY VINEYARDS & BISHOP'S PEAK WINES

Farming has been a way of life at Talley Vineyards for more than half a century. In 1948, the Oliver Talley family began growing specialty vegetables in the Arroyo Grande Valley. In later years, they became grape growers as they realized the potential for cultivating premium varietals on the steep hillsides above their fields.

In 1982, the Talleys planted their first vines on a small plot of land that four years later produced 450 cases of wine. Today, Talley Vineyards has 130 acres of vines and an annual production of 14,000 cases of single-vineyard, estate-bottled Chardonnay and Pinot Noir.

Talley Vineyards comprises four vineyards: the Rincon Vineyard, planted adjacent to the winery; Rosemary's Vineyard, located one mile to the west; and Oliver's Vineyard and Stone Corral Vineyard, both located in the neighboring Edna Valley. The distinctive wines from these vineyards reflect the unique character of the soil where the grapes are grown.

The Talley winemaking team uses traditional, Burgundian "non-interventionist" methods to create award-winning wines. Native yeasts are used in fermentation, all Chardonnay is barrel fermented, and most of the wines are bottled without filtration.

But Talley Vineyards feels that there is more to making wine than superior grapes and time-proven techniques. Talley believes that "the human interaction with the soil" is an important factor, and recognizes the invaluable role its many longtime employees play in the quality of Talley's wines.

In 1997, Talley Vineyards created "Bishop's Peak," its "growers' label," as an acknowledgment of the grape farmer's vital contribution to the finished wine. Grapes for Bishop's Peak are purchased throughout San Luis Obispo County from farmers who, like the Talleys, have a commitment to growing select grapes by using sustainable farming practices. The primary varietals for Bishop's Peak vintages are Chardonnay, Pinot Noir, Syrah, and Cabernet Sauvignon.

Talley Vineyards & Bishop's Peak Wines
3031 Lopez Drive
Arroyo Grande, CA 93420
(805) 489-0446
info@talleyvineyards.com
www.talleyvineyards.com

Sub-AVA: Arroyo Grande Valley

Owners: Don, Rosemary, Brian, and Johnine Talley

Tasting Hours:
10:30 a.m. – 4:30 p.m. daily

Wines: Chardonnay, Pinot Noir, Syrah, Cabernet Sauvignon, Riesling

Winemaker's Specialty:
Estate Pinot Noir

Winemaker: Steve Rasmussen

Roast Salmon with Beet Vinaigrette

4 5-oz. pieces of salmon
Salt and freshly ground pepper to taste
1 Tbsp. Italian parsley, finely minced
3 medium beets
1 shallot, minced
Juice and zest of 2 lemons, minced
1 sprig of thyme
3/4 c. virgin olive oil

Sprinkle salmon with salt, pepper, and parsley. Arrange fish in a baking dish and set aside. Preheat oven to 425°. Place beets in a baking pan with a small amount of water, cover, and roast about 45 minutes until skins peel off easily. Cool, peel, and dice. Place shallot, minced zest, juice, and thyme in a small bowl and let macerate for 20 minutes. Whisk in olive oil and add beets and salt and pepper to taste. Let mixture marry for 30 minutes. Heat oven to 450° and roast salmon for 8 to 10 minutes. Serve immediately with beet vinaigrette and **Talley Vineyards Chardonnay.**

TOLOSA WINERY

Tolosa Winery's vintages reflect the labor and care of a 200-year-old winemaking tradition reaching back to the days of Early California and the Mission San Luis Obispo de Tolosa's Franciscan padres. With complete control over its vineyards and winemaking practices, Tolosa produces handcrafted, artisan wines using minimal manipulation and filtration and gentle racking to bring out the "personality" of each vintage.

Tolosa's beginnings date back to 1986, when friends and law partners Robin Baggett and Bob Schiebelhut began making wine in Bob's barn with locally purchased grapes. In 1990, Robin and Bob began planting Tolosa's estate vineyards, which now total more than 700 acres in the Edna Valley. Vineyard manager Jim Efird joined the partnership in 1998, the same year Tolosa constructed its high-tech-style winery and released its first vintage.

Like the Burgundy region of France, the Edna Valley offers grape growers special soils and climate that together provide exceptional conditions for cultivating grapes of extraordinary character. Warm days, cool nights, and the "challenging" Edna Valley land produce a low-yield crop that lingers on the vine longer and develops intense flavors.

At harvest, winemaker Ed Filice has the advantage of choosing among different blocks and rows of grapes to find just the right fruit to match the style of wine he wants to make. Each row is individually hand harvested, processed, and aged for one year in French oak barrels. Then Robin, Bob, Jim, and Ed sample each wine to determine which rows have developed unique characteristics that further emphasize the *terroir*. They then select which wines to blend together to make the year's vintage. When a certain area of the vineyard is deemed exceptional, those wines are bottled under Tolosa's "1772" select label.

Since bottling its first vintage, Tolosa has garnered numerous awards: The 1999 Pinot Noir won the "Best Pinot Noir of California" at the California State Fair Wine Competition; the 2000 Chardonnay won the "Best New World Chardonnay" at the Jerry Mead International Wine Competition; and the 2001 Pinot Noir "1772" received 92 points from *Wine Enthusiast* magazine.

Tolosa Winery
4910 Edna Road
San Luis Obispo, CA 93401
(805) 782-0300
(866) 782-0300 toll free
info@tolosawinery.com
www.tolosawinery.com

Sub-AVA: Edna Valley

Owners: Robin Baggett, Jim Efird, Bob Schiebelhut

Tasting Hours:
10 a.m. – 5 p.m. daily

Wines: Chardonnay, Pinot Noir, Syrah

Winemaker's Specialty:
"1772" select wines

Winemaker: Ed Filice

Chicken with Mushrooms and Sweetbreads

2-3/4 lb. free-range chicken
1 c. Tolosa Estate Chardonnay
1 each small onion, carrot, celery stalk, leek,
  bouquet garni
2 to 3 cabbage leaves
14 oz. sweetbreads (lamb or veal)
10 oz. mushrooms, quartered
6 Tbsp. unsalted butter
Juice of 1/2 lemon
4 Tbsp. flour
2 egg yolks
4 Tbsp. crème fraîche
12 puffed pastry shells, pre-baked (optional)
Salt and freshly ground pepper

Place chicken, wine, carrot, onion, celery, leek, bouquet garni, cabbage, salt, and pepper in a stockpot and cover with water. Bring to a boil, then simmer for 35 minutes, until chicken is tender. Add sweetbreads for the last 15 minutes of cooking time. Remove chicken and sweetbreads, discard vegetables, and reserve stock. Skin and bone chicken and cut into bite-size pieces. Skin sweetbreads, remove membrane and break into small pieces. Sauté mushrooms in 2 Tbsp. butter, lemon juice, and salt and pepper. Melt remaining butter in a large saucepan and stir in flour. Add 2-2/3 cups of stock; stir vigorously as it comes to a boil. Thin if necessary with a little more stock. Simmer for 10 minutes. Stir in chicken, sweetbreads, and mushrooms, and simmer briefly. Remove from heat. Stir in egg yolks and crème fraîche. Spoon into puff pastry shells. Serve with **Tolosa Pinot Noir**.
Recipe courtesy Ed Filice, winemaker, Tolosa Winery

WOLFF VINEYARDS

At Wolff Vineyards, "Wine tasting isn't just a destination, it's an experience," insist winery owners Jean-Pierre and Elke Wolff. They invite their guests not only to taste their current releases but to commune with nature and "connect" with their ecologically friendly vineyard.

The wine-tasting experience begins at Wolff Vineyards' beautiful outdoor tasting area, which is surrounded by a panorama of the Edna Valley's rolling hills and vineyards. Located on land bordered by two ocean-bound creeks, Wolff Vineyards has a strong commitment to maintaining and improving the ecology of its unique site. Conservation programs provide a natural habitat for quail, kestrel, red-tail hawks, barn owls, and golden eagles, along with habitat restoration for migratory fish. Jean-Pierre and Elke encourage their guests to bring picnic lunches and spend the day exploring the many hiking trails throughout the vineyard.

Jean-Pierre and Elke founded Wolff Vineyards in 1999 when they purchased the 125-acre property, which was originally planted in the early 1970s by Andy MacGregor, one of the area's pioneer grape growers. The Wolffs expanded the vineyard to include 55 acres of Chardonnay grapes, 37 of Pinot Noir, and 13 of Teroldego, Syrah, Petit Syrah, and Riesling. They also added an artisan winery.

In its continued commitment to protect and improve the land's ecosystem, Wolff Vineyards uses sustainable farming practices to grow the choice grapes that are turned into award-winning wine. Although most of Wolff Vineyards' grapes are sold to "ultra-premium" winemakers, Jean-Pierre carefully selects designated blocks to produce small quantities—less than 5,000 cases per year—of handcrafted wines.

Jean-Pierre maintains a focus on blending Burgundian-style winemaking methods with New World, estate-grown grapes. "This technique," he says, "gives each vintage a well-balanced flavor and site-specific *terroir* characteristics." The quality of Wolff Vineyards' wines also reflects Jean-Pierre's close attention to detail in his winemaking methods, which include barrel fermentation *sur lie*, *batonnage*, hand punch-down, and partial carbonic maceration.

Jean-Pierre wants Wolff Vineyards to remain an artisan winery and has no desire to "grow the business" into a large-scale production facility. He explains that if he can't personally control the consistency and quality of his wines, he doesn't want to produce them. He believes a winemaker's style reflects his personality, and that the accomplished winemaker doesn't rest on past laurels but continually strives "to raise the bar" for next year's vintages.

Wolff Vineyards
6238 Orcutt Road
San Luis Obispo, CA 93401
(805) 781-0448
jp.wolff@wolffvineyards.com
www.wolffvineyards.com

Sub-AVA: Edna Valley

Owners:
Jean-Pierre and Elke Wolff

Hours:
11 a.m. – 5 p.m. Saturday – Sunday
And holidays

Wines: Old-Vine Chardonnay, Pinot Noir, Teroldego, Syrah, Petite Syrah, Riesling

Winemaker's Specialty:
Old-Vine Chardonnay

Winemaker:
Jean-Pierre Wolff

Baked Salmon with Goat Cheese and Fresh Rosemary

6 salmon filets (6 to 7 oz. each)
1/4 c. fresh lemon juice
1/4 tsp. salt
1/4 tsp. freshly ground pepper
6 Tbsp. olive oil
2 cloves garlic, crushed
6 oz. soft, creamy goat cheese, room temperature
6 Tbsp. fresh rosemary

Place salmon filets in a shallow baking dish. Mix lemon juice, salt, and pepper in a small bowl and gradually whisk in oil. Mix in garlic. Pour over fish. Cover and refrigerate for 2 hours, turning fish several times. Heat oven to 450°. Place fish, skin side down, on a greased baking sheet and bake 9 to 12 minutes. Meanwhile, beat cheese until soft and smooth and mix with 3 Tbsp. rosemary. Remove fish from oven when done, discard skin, and transfer filets to a platter. Season with salt and pepper to taste. Place a generous dollop of the cheese mixture on top of each fillet. Sprinkle with remaining rosemary. Serve with **Wolff Vineyards Old-Vine Chardonnay.**

SAN LUIS OBISPO COASTAL
WINE TRAIL

ALAPAY CELLARS

BAILEYANA

CERRO CALIENTE

CLAIBORNE & CHURCHILL

DOMAINE ALFRED

EDNA VALLEY VINEYARD

KELSEY SEE CANYON VINEYARDS

KYNSI WINERY

LAETITIA VINEYARD

TALLEY VINEYARDS

TOLOSA WINERY

SAUCELITO CANYON

WINDEMERE

WOLFF VINEYARDS

CENTRAL COAST

VINEYARD TEAM

PROMOTING
SUSTAINABLE
VINEYARD
PRACTICES.

Biological Farming Project

SYRAH CT

CAMINO EDNA

DUST
KILLS
VINES!
15 MPH

WILD HORSE WINERY CT

WINERIES →

CHARDONNAY ROAD

ZINFANDEL

DUNNING VINEYARDS
← 11 MILES

WINDWARD VINEYARD
8 MILES

WILD HORSE WINERY
6 MILES

VISTA DEL REY
← 18 MILES

CARMODY McNIGHT
← 18 MILES

MIDNIGHT CELLARS
← 9 MILES

SYLVESTER WINERY
← 14 MILES

VINEYARD DR

"Wine is light, held together by water." —Galileo (1564-1642)

Pipestone Vineyards, Paso Robles   *(Photo by Karl Wang)*

Page 52: Wine country signs   *(Photos by Janet Penn Franks)*

Laetitia Vineyard & Winery, Arroyo Grande
(Photo courtesy Laetitia Vineyard & Winery)

The vineyards of Doce Robles and Summerwood, Paso Robles
(Photo by Janet Penn Franks)

"A glass of wine is great refreshment after a hard day's work." —Beethoven (1770-1827)

(Photo by Karl Wang)

Photo opposite page: Spring wildflowers in the Edna Valley at the base of Islay Hill, one of the Seven Sisters dormant volcanos   (Photo by Janet Penn Franks)

"Wine brightens the life and thinking of anyone." —Thomas Jefferson (1743-1826)

PASO ROBLES
AREA WINERIES

"A waltz and a glass of wine invite an encore." —Johann Strauss (1825-1899)

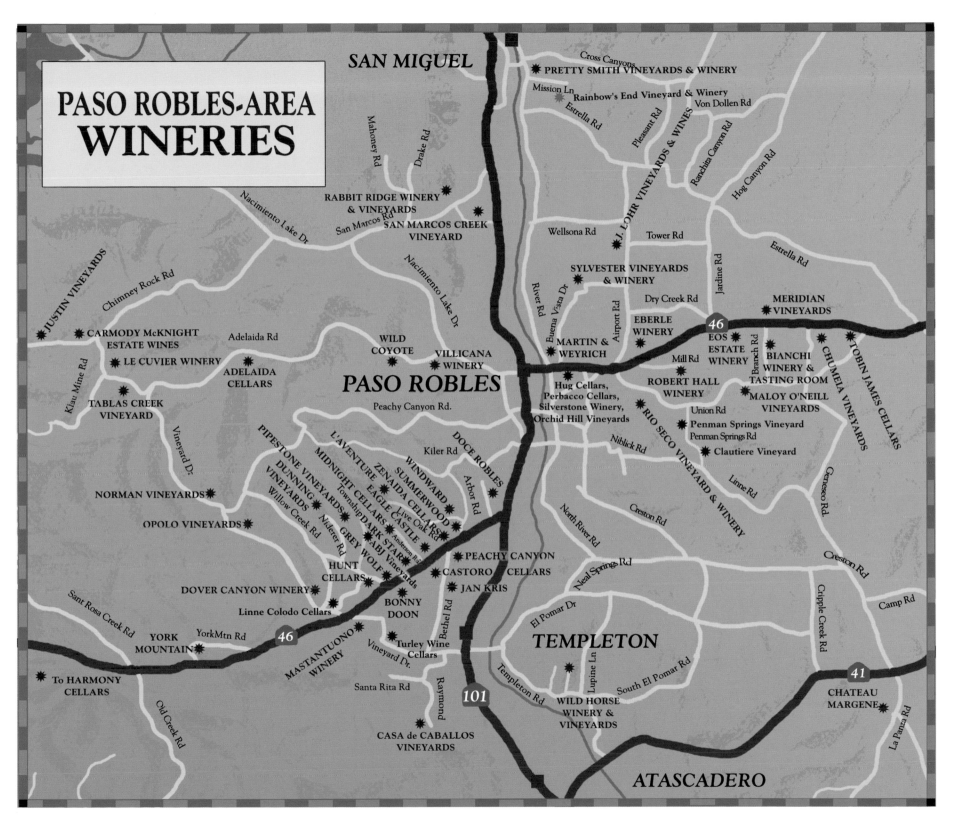

PASO ROBLES-AREA WINERIES

SAN MIGUEL

Cross Canyons

✷ PRETTY SMITH VINEYARDS & WINERY

Mission Ln

Rainbow's End Vineyard & Winery

Von Dollen Rd

Mahoney Rd

Drake Rd

Estrella Rd

Pleasant Rd

Ranchita Canyon Rd

Hog Canyon Rd

Nacimiento Lake Dr

RABBIT RIDGE WINERY
& VINEYARDS

San Marcos Rd

SAN MARCOS CREEK
VINEYARD

Wellsona Rd

Tower Rd

Estrella Rd

Nacimiento Lake Dr

JUSTIN VINEYARDS

Chimney Rock Rd

SYLVESTER VINEYARDS
& WINERY

Dry Creek Rd

Jardine Rd

MERIDIAN
VINEYARDS

CARMODY McKNIGHT
ESTATE WINES

Adelaida Rd

WILD
COYOTE

River Rd

Buena Vista Dr

Airport Rd

EBERLE
WINERY

46

EOS
ESTATE
WINERY

BIANCHI
WINERY &
TASTING ROOM

Klau Mine Rd

LE CUVIER WINERY

ADELAIDA
CELLARS

VILLICANA
WINERY

PASO ROBLES

MARTIN &
WEYRICH

Mill Rd

ROBERT HALL
WINERY

CHUMEIA VINEYARDS

TOBIN JAMES CELLARS

TABLAS CREEK
VINEYARD

Peachy Canyon Rd.

Hug Cellars,
Perbacco Cellars,
Silverstone Winery,
Orchid Hill Vineyards

MALOY O'NEILL
VINEYARDS

Vineyard Dr

Union Rd

Penman Springs Vineyard

Penman Springs Rd

PIPESTONE VINEYARDS

L'AVENTURE

Kiler Rd

DOCE
ROBLES

Niblick Rd

RIO SECO VINEYARD & WINERY

Clautiere Vineyard

Linne Rd

Geneseo Rd

NORMAN VINEYARDS

MIDNIGHT CELLARS

ZENAIDA CELLARS

SUMMERWOOD

WINDWARD

Arbor Rd

Creston Rd

DUNNING
VIINEYARDS

Township

EAGLE CASTLE

Live Oak Rd

North River Rd

OPOLO VINEYARDS

Willow Creek Rd

Niderer Rd

GREY WOLF

DARK STAR

Anderson Rd

ABJ Vineyards

HUNT
CELLARS

PEACHY CANYON
CELLARS

DOVER CANYON WINERY

CASTORO
CELLARS

Neal Springs Rd

Creston Rd

Linne Colodo Cellars

JAN KRIS

Sant Rosa Creek Rd

BONNY
DOON

Bethel Rd

El Pomar Dr

Camp Rd

YORK
MOUNTAIN

YorkMtn Rd

46

MASTANTUONO
WINERY

Vineyard Dr.

Turley Wine
Cellars

TEMPLETON

Lupine Ln

South El Pomar Rd

Cripple Creek Rd

To HARMONY
CELLARS

Santa Rita Rd

Raymond

101

Templeton Rd

WILD HORSE
WINERY &
VINEYARDS

41

CHATEAU
MARGENE

Old Creek Rd

CASA de CABALLOS
VINEYARDS

ATASCADERO

La Panza Rd

Pages 58-59: The vineyards of Summerwood Winery, Paso Robles   *(Photo by Janet Penn Franks)*
Photo opposite page: Scenic wildflowers along Highway 46 West, Paso Robles   *(Photo by Janet Penn Franks)*

ADELAIDA CELLARS

Located 16 miles from the Pacific Ocean in the hills west of Paso Robles, Adelaida Cellars derives its name from the nearby 1870s pioneer town. The winery was established in 1981 and purchased in 1991 by the Van Steenwyk family, who produce site-specific wines from two estate vineyards. The Van Steenwyks believe the geographical features of their HMR and Viking Estate vineyards are ideal for producing grapes of extraordinary character.

Adelaida Cellars' vineyards lie in a narrow strip of coastal land where clay soils are intermixed with calcareous and fractured shale. The terrain not only offers a high nutrient value but also readily absorbs and retains moisture and requires only minimal irrigation. Rare in California, these soils are similar to those found in the Burgundy and northern Rhône Valley regions of France.

Planted in 1963, HMR Estate Vineyard boasts San Luis Obispo County's oldest Pinot Noir vines. The mountaintop vineyard has an elevation of 1,700 feet and lies fully exposed to the vagaries of Central Coast weather, but Adelaida Cellars has had great success in cultivating the fragile varietal in these harsh climatic conditions. In 2003, the Van Steenwyks planted the upper slopes of the mountain with 18 acres of Syrah, propagated on rootstock well suited to the low acidity of the limestone soil. Elizabeth Van Steenwyk points

out, "This world-class vineyard is located in what *Wine Spectator* magazine calls the Rhône Zone, a part of west Paso Robles that produces big, bold Syrah wines."

Adelaida's Viking Estate Vineyard grows within the property's warmer microclimate. Planted in 1991 at an elevation of 1,600 feet, the vineyard is flanked by two adjoining mountain ridges that provide shelter from the elements. The Van Steenwyks refer to the Viking vineyard as "Cabernet country" because of its warm, dry climate and lean mountain soils, as well as its long growing season that is ideally suited for producing Cabernet Sauvignon grapes.

Adelaida Cellars
5805 Adelaida Road
Paso Robles, CA 93446
(805) 239-8980
wines@adelaida.com
www.adelaida.com

Sub-AVA: Paso Robles

Owners:
The Van Steenwyk family

Tasting Hours:
11 a.m. – 5 p.m. daily

Wines: Cabernet Sauvignon, Syrah, Zinfandel, Pinot Noir, Chardonnay, Viognier

Winemaker's Specialties:
Pinot Noir, Syrah, Viognier

Winemaker: Terry Culton

Adelaida Pan-Roasted Almonds

8 oz. Adelaida (or other) almonds, blanched
Dash of olive oil
1 small dried chili, finely diced (optional)
1 clove garlic, finely diced (optional)
2 generous pinches sea salt to taste, preferably coarse-ground

Blanch almonds in boiling water for one minute to loosen the pellicle (brown skin). Rinse with cold water and drain. Pop white meat from pellicle by pinching the end with finger and thumb. Add the olive oil, chili, and garlic (if you wish), and almonds to a hot, nonstick pan. Pan roast over medium heat, tossing occasionally until almonds are golden brown on both sides. As the almonds brown, add sea salt. Serve immediately in a ramekin or on a plate, adding more sea salt as desired. Serve with **Adelaida Cellars Chardonnay, HMR Estate,** or **Vin Gris.**

BIANCHI WINERY & TASTING ROOM

Bianchi Winery & Tasting Room is one of Paso Robles' newest wineries, but owner Glenn Bianchi is anything but new to the winery business. Glenn's winemaking history dates back to 1974, when he and his father, Joseph, operated a large-scale commercial winery in Kerman, Calif. "The building was just a shell when we started," remembers Glenn, "and the first thing we did was bring in all new, modern, quality equipment."

After Joseph passed away, Glenn decided to change his winemaking style. He now produces high-quality varietals with an emphasis on what he calls "a boutique attitude at the winery." Glenn had a specific reason when he chose Paso Robles for his new business venture. "The area is known for great reds," Glenn explains. "This is where the competition is for Napa and Sonoma."

As in his days at the Kerman winery, Glenn says he is dedicated to quality in all aspects of his winemaking business and that he spared no expense in building Bianchi Winery & Tasting Room. The state-of-the-art facility has only top-of-the-line equipment, including a 150,000-gallon winery with its own bottling line.

Bianchi's 40-acre vineyard produces Cabernet Sauvignon, Zinfandel, Merlot, and Syrah grapes for its estate-wine label, Heritage. The winery sources fruit for its other varietals from select vineyards in the Central Coast AVA, with an emphasis on the Paso Robles area.

Bianchi features what Glenn describes as "a California/New Wave-style" tasting room, with a kitchen, barbeque area, conference room, gift shop, and fireplace, and floor-to-ceiling windows that maximize the view of the Merlot vineyard and the spectacular sunsets. Outside, a small lake (stocked with bass and bluegill), a waterfall, a gazebo, and a patio provide a refreshing, relaxing atmosphere for sipping Bianchi's current releases and enjoying special events.

Winemaker Steve Felten brings to Bianchi experience and expertise—Steve earned a bachelor's degree in microbiology from California State University, Northridge, and a master's in enology from California State University, Fresno, and worked at large wineries in the Central Valley and at boutique wineries in Napa and Sonoma. Before joining Bianchi, for nine years he was the director of winemaking at neighboring EOS Estate Winery.

Bianchi Winery & Tasting Room
3380 Branch Road
Paso Robles, CA 93446
(805) 226-9922
sales@bianchiwine.com
www.bianchiwine.com

Sub-AVA: Paso Robles

Owner: Glenn Bianchi

Tasting Hours:
10 a.m. – 5 p.m. daily

Wines: Zinfandel, Cabernet Sauvignon, Merlot, Chardonnay, Sauvignon Blanc, Petite Sirah, Pinot Noir, Pinot Grigio, Syrah

Winemaker's Specialties: Zinfandel, Cabernet Sauvignon, Merlot

Winemaker: Steve Felten

Italian Sausage and Peppers

1/4 c. olive oil
8 links spicy Italian sausage
1 each red pepper and onion, sliced
6 cloves garlic, chopped
1/4 tsp. chili flakes
2 tsp. fresh rosemary, chopped
1/4 c. fresh parsley, chopped
3/4 c. Bianchi Chardonnay
14-1/2-oz. can Italian plum tomatoes
1/2 tsp. each salt and pepper

In a large skillet, brown sausage on all sides in 2 Tbsp. olive oil over medium-high heat. Remove, cut into thirds, and keep warm. Add pepper to skillet and cook over high heat until lightly browned. Remove and keep warm with sausage. Place remaining olive oil into skillet, reducing heat to medium. Add onion, garlic, chili flakes, rosemary, and 2 Tbsp. parsley. Cook until onion is tender. Add Chardonnay, stirring to dislodge browned bits from bottom of the skillet. Continue cooking until the liquid is reduced. Add tomatoes with their juice, salt, and pepper, and cook 7 to 8 minutes. Return sausage and peppers to pan, bring to a boil, then simmer until the sausage is cooked through and sauce has thickened, about 15 minutes. Serve over polenta or pasta and sprinkle with remaining parsley. Serve with **Bianchi Cabernet Sauvignon**.

BONNY DOON VINEYARD

Although Bonny Doon Vineyard is a Santa Cruz-based winery, its Paso Robles tasting room is a popular spot with wine tasters, as well as with gardeners, herbalists, and chefs. Located at Sycamore Farms on Highway 46 West, Bonny Doon's tasting room offers not only blended varietals and a shady lawn picnic area, but also a wide selection of unusual herbs and interesting gift items for plant lovers and gourmets.

Bonny Doon is the brainchild of Randall Graham, a fun-loving enology graduate of the University of California, Davis, and his zany sense of humor is reflected in the winery's philosophy, marketing, and packaging. Randall describes his winemaking as "incorrigibly eclectic." Dozens of Old World varieties—including Syrah, Grenache, Mourvèdre, Cinsault, Viognier, Muscat, Zinfandel, and Riesling—are blended to create Bonny Doon's Rhône- and Italian-style varietals.

Grapes sourced from select Paso Robles vineyards and fruit from Randall's own estate vineyard in Monterey County produce many of the winery's distinctive selections. Randall's humorous approach to marketing is reflected in the naming of his "Big House Red" blend—the grapes are grown on his Monterey County Ca' del Solo Vineyard, which lies adjacent to the Salinas Valley State Prison, Soledad. The vineyard's location also provides the setting for the amusing tale of the wine's development, a prison escape story that is printed on the bottle's front and back labels. All Bonny Doon labels feature renditions of original artwork by well-known artists, including cartoonist and illustrator Ralph Steadman.

Although Randall's home ground is Santa Cruz, he explains, "The world is my vineyard." Through numerous partnerships, Bonny Doon produces wines in France, southern Italy, and Germany. Randall makes many trips abroad each year to keep careful watch over his European winemaking.

Bonny Doon Vineyard
2485 Highway 46 West
Paso Robles, CA 93446
(805) 239-5614
grahmcru@bonnydoonvineyard.com
www.bonnydoonvineyard.com

Owner: Randall Graham

Tasting Hours:
10 a.m. – 5 p.m. daily

Wines: Rhône-style red blends, Syrah, Barbera, Sangiovese, Zinfandel, Charbono, Tannat, Dry Riesling, Rosé, white blends, dessert wines

Winemaker's Specialties:
Rhône- and Italian-style varietals

Winemaker: Randall Graham

Big House Beef Stew

6 lbs. boneless beef shoulder, cut into 1-inch cubes
1/3 c. olive oil, divided in half
Salt, pepper, and fresh oregano, chopped (to taste)
3 large cloves garlic, minced
1 c. each onion and celery, coarsely chopped
25 small white pearl onions, peeled
2 c. Bonny Doon Vineyard Big House Red wine
1 bay leaf
1/2 tsp. fresh thyme, chopped
1 Tbsp. arrowroot
1/2 c. water
30 green olives, pitted and blanched
Zest of 1 lemon, finely julienned

Heat half of olive oil in a Dutch oven, add beef, sprinkle with salt, pepper, and oregano, and brown. Stir in garlic, onions, and celery, and continue cooking over medium heat until onions are transparent. Add enough water to just cover meat and vegetables, and bake at 350° for 1/2 hour. Remove from oven, set aside. In a skillet, sauté pearl onions in remaining olive oil until browned. Add pearl onions, wine, bay leaf, and thyme to meat. Stir. Cover Dutch oven and simmer stew over low heat until meat is tender. In a small bowl, mix arrowroot with 1/2 cup water until smooth. Stir into stew. Bring stew to a boil over high heat, stirring constantly, until slightly thickened. Stir in olives and lemon zest. Serve with **Bonny Doon Big House Red**.
Recipe courtesy Patti Ballard, food and wine writer and resident chef, Bonny Doon Vineyard

CARMODY McKNIGHT ESTATE WINES

The beauty of Carmody McKnight Estate Wines' exquisitely landscaped grounds is rivaled only by the stunning wine labels themselves. Each vibrantly colored label depicts a scene of vineyard life painted by artist Gary Carmody Conway, the winery's owner and a screen actor, director, and writer.

Gary's move to the west hills of Paso Robles began as a family retreat and an inspiration for his art. In the late 1960s, Gary and his wife, Marian McKnight Conway—a former Miss America—purchased 320 acres in Adelaida, six miles from the Pacific Ocean. Entranced by the beauty of the terrain and the property's circa-1860s pioneer farmhouse, the Conways and their daughter, Kathleen, at first commuted on weekends from their Los Angeles home. In the ensuing years, as the region began to capture the attention of vintners and wine lovers around the world, Gary and Marian became interested in viticulture and winemaking, and started a family business destined for success.

In 1985, the Conways planted their first grapevines in the limestone and volcanic soils of the property's south-facing slopes. Four years later, they produced their first wine in the cellar of their farmhouse. The name "Carmody McKnight"—a blending of Gary and Marian's birth names—was created at the bottling of the 1995 vintage. Soon, Kathleen joined her parents as an owner of Carmody McKnight Estate Wines. In 2005, the straw-bale winery was constructed with 24-inch-thick walls that allow for natural cooling and humidity control.

From the beginning, Carmody McKnight has focused on growing optimum-quality grapes. Gary, Marian, and Kathleen feel that the uniqueness of the soil transfers to the wine and the grapes embody the *terroir* of the land. "Our soils are so extraordinary that they are the subject of several long-term studies being conducted by California Polytechnic State University, John Deere Corporation, Motorola, and Earth IT," says Gary. Winemaker Greg Cropper explains that his winemaking style originates in the vineyard and continues in the winery. "The use of French oak barrels is kept to a minimum, so the flavor of the fruit isn't masked," he says.

At the tasting room—which is inside the old farmhouse—wine aficionados can sample Carmody McKnight's selection of wines, browse the gift shop and art gallery that offer Gary's artwork and book, *Art of the Vineyard*, and purchase estate-bottled olive oil from trees that grow on the property. Guests are invited to picnic at tables beside the ponds in which lilies and lotus flowers grow, and to enjoy this exceptionally beautiful winery.

Carmody McKnight Estate Wines
11240 Chimney Rock Road
Paso Robles, CA 93446
(805) 238-9392
carmodymcknight@thegrid.net
www.carmodymcknight.com

Sub-AVA: Paso Robles

Owners: Gary Carmody Conway, Marian McKnight Conway, Kathleen Conway

Tasting Hours:
10 a.m. – 5 p.m. daily

Wines: Cabernet Sauvignon, Merlot, Cabernet Franc, Chardonnay, Pinot Noir, Meritage blends, sparkling wine, dessert wines

Winemaker's Specialties: Cadenza, Cabernet Franc

Winemaker: Greg Cropper

Prosciutto and Gruyere Pastry Pinwheels

1 sheet frozen puff pastry, thawed
4 oz. thinly sliced prosciutto
2 Tbsp. fresh basil, chopped
3/4 c. (packed) finely grated Gruyere cheese
1 egg, beaten

Cut pastry in half to form two 9- by 4-inch rectangles. Arrange half of prosciutto on one piece of pastry, leaving a 1/2-inch border along one 9-inch side. Sprinkle with half of basil and cheese. Brush border with egg. Starting with the 9-inch side without the border, roll pastry jellyroll style and press gently to seal along edge. Wrap in plastic wrap. Repeat with remaining pastry, prosciutto, basil, and cheese. Refrigerate until firm, at least 3 hours and no longer than 2 days. Cut logs crosswise in 1/2-inch-thick slices and place 1 inch apart on 2 large baking sheets lined with parchment paper. Bake one sheet at a time at 400° for about 16 minutes, until golden brown. Serve with **Carmody McKnight Marian's Vineyard Chardonnay**.

CASA DE CABALLOS VINEYARDS

At the end of a tree-lined road in west Templeton, a novel surprise awaits wine tasters—Casa de Caballos Vineyards, where owners Tom and Sheila Morgan display their twin passions for producing fine wines and prize Arabian horses. In a tranquil setting of vineyards and pastures, the Morgans invite visitors to bring a picnic lunch and sample current releases, pet newborn foals, and enjoy a day in the country. Templeton physician Tom Morgan's interest in winemaking began as a hobby, when he made fruit and berry wines in his free time while attending medical school in Southern California. After graduation, Tom moved to Templeton and purchased the 33-acre property that is today known as Casa de Caballos—in Spanish, "House of the Horses"—Vineyards.

In 1982, Tom, his wife, Sheila, and three of their sons planted one acre of Pinot Noir and White Riesling vines. Later, they added Muscat, Canelli, Merlot, and Cabernet Sauvignon, expanding their vineyard to six acres. It was then, as the Morgans' vineyard grew in size, that Sheila began breeding Arabian horses.

Today, Casa de Caballos is known nationally and internationally for both award-winning wine and champion Arabians. The winery makes seven wines, 99 percent of which are sold exclusively at its tasting room and through the wine club. Several vintages are served at select North County restaurants.

Casa de Caballos wines—most selections are named after Sheila's Arabian mares—have received numerous awards. Most recently, the Morgans' 2001 Forgetmenot received a gold medal for Best of Class in the 2004 Jerry Mead New World International Wine Competition. In 2003, the Morgans' 2002 Periwinkle Pinot Noir garnered a rating of 91 points at the 2003 Affairs of the Vine Pinot Noir Shootout.

In addition to wine, Casa de Caballos' Under the Eaves Gift Shop offers an extensive selection of wine accessories, glassware, logoed clothing, gourmet food items, greeting cards, and walnuts from the Morgans' orchard.

The winery's patio and lawn area offer sweeping views of the Paso Robles Valley and Templeton, a perfect place to relax and sip a glass of wine, and a venue available for special gatherings and small weddings. Events may also be hosted in the winery's large barrel room, which is paneled with 80-year-old barn wood. Complete outdoor kitchen facilities and a barbeque pit are available.

Casa de Caballos Vineyards
2225 Raymond Avenue
Templeton, CA 93465
(805) 434-1687
info@casadecaballos.com
www.casadecaballos.com

Sub-AVA: Paso Robles

Owners: Tom and Sheila Morgan

Tasting Hours:
11 a.m. – 5 p.m. daily

Wines: Pinot Noir, Riesling, Cabernet Sauvignon, Merlot

Winemaker's Specialty:
Pinot Noir

Winemaker: Tom Morgan

Casa de Caballos Vineyards Lemon Chicken

6 boneless chicken breast halves
Lemon juice
1 stick butter
1 c. flour
1 c. Romano cheese, grated
1 tsp. garlic salt

Pound chicken breasts until fairly flat. Place in a container with a lid and completely cover chicken with lemon juice. Marinate for at least 4 hours. Melt butter on a cookie sheet with sides in a 375° oven. Mix flour, cheese, and garlic salt in a container. Dredge chicken breasts, one at a time, in flour mixture. Place on cookie sheet with melted butter, turning breasts so both sides are coated with butter. Sprinkle with some of remaining flour mixture. Bake approximately 40 minutes until golden brown. Serve with **Casa de Caballos Pinot Noir**.

CASTORO CELLARS

Castoro Cellars, one of the oldest wineries in the Paso Robles area, was founded by husband-and-wife team Niels and Berit "Bimmer" Udsen with a simple concept in mind: Everyone should be able to enjoy a high-quality bottle of wine at the evening meal and not have to pay "half a day's wages" for it.

Niels and Bimmer's winery began as a "backyard" winemaking business in 1983, producing small lots of wine for the Udsens' family and friends. Showcasing their sense of humor, the Udsens named their winery "Castoro"—Italian for "Beaver"—which is Niels' longtime nickname and inspired Castoro Cellars' motto: "Dam Fine Wine."

As the '80s became the '90s, the demand for Castoro Cellars wine had become so great that in 1991 the Udsens acquired 200 acres in Paso Robles on which they planted a vineyard and built a winery. In addition, Niels and Bimmer purchased several existing vineyards in the surrounding area. Today, Castoro Cellars ranks as one of the largest wineries in the United States, producing small lots of most varietals and larger quantities of a few selected vintages.

Outdoor enthusiasts, Niels and Bimmer are avid stewards of the environment and use sustainable farming techniques. Some of their habitat-friendly practices include the release of predatory insects for pest control and the use of pomace—semi-composted grape-skin and -seed residue—for weed control and fertilization. "Growing up in Denmark, we had a strong environmental awareness," explains Bimmer. "When we planted our organic vineyards, we did it because it was the right thing to do."

Castoro Cellars' tasting room, patio, and events room are not to be missed. A 100-foot-long grape arbor leads to the Mediterranean-style tasting room stocked with wine accessories, freshly canned jellies and jams, rich marinades, spices, and handmade jewelry. A canopy of trees shades the attractively landscaped patio and lawn area, where, during balmy summer evenings, internationally known musicians perform outdoor concerts. Guests can relax, enjoy the spectacular view of the surrounding vineyards, and purchase locally prepared gourmet meals for the ultimate picnic as they take in a special musical experience. In the winter, the concerts move indoors to the nearby events room, which offers a revolving exhibit of paintings by local artists.

Castoro Cellars
1315 N. Bethel Road
Templeton, CA 93465
(805) 238-0725
(888) 326-3463 toll free
tastingroom@castorocellars.com
www.castorocellars.com

Sub-AVA: Paso Robles

Owners: Niels and Berit Udsen

Tasting Hours:
10 a.m. – 5:30 p.m. daily

Wines: Cabernet Sauvignon, Zinfandel, Pinot Noir, Chardonnay, Fume Blanc, Viognier, Syrah, Tempranillo, Merlot, Muscat Canelli, Petite Sirah

Winemaker's Specialties: Cabernet Sauvignon, Zinfandel

Winemaker: Tom Myers

Portuguese-Style Scallops

1-1/2 lbs. scallops
1/2 tsp. salt
1/4 tsp. pepper
1 Tbsp. olive oil, divided
1/3 c. Castoro Cellars Late Harvest Zinfandel
2 Tbsp. fresh lemon juice
5 cloves garlic, chopped
1/4 c. chopped fresh parsley, divided
2 c. long-grain rice, cooked

Sprinkle scallops with salt and pepper. Heat 1-1/2 tsp. oil in skillet over high heat for about 3 minutes. Add half of the scallops and cook about 2 minutes on each side until browned. Remove scallops from pan and keep warm. Repeat procedure using the rest of the scallops, remove from pan, and keep warm. Add wine and lemon juice to pan, scraping browned bits from the pan. Add scallops, garlic, and 3 Tbsp. parsley, and sauté 30 seconds over high heat. Serve scallops over rice and sprinkle with remaining parsley. Serve with **Castoro Cellars Late Harvest Zinfandel**.

CHATEAU MARGENE

Just a scenic, 18-minute drive east of Highway 101, Chateau Margene is dedicated to the production of small lots of luxury, handcrafted Cabernet Sauvignon wines. Michael and Margene Mooney, proprietors of the family-owned boutique winery, share a love of wine and a desire to further Paso Robles' reputation as a world-class wine region.

In 1992, the Mooneys' curiosity about the wines of the Paso Robles sub-AVA brought them to the Paso Robles Wine Festival. Impressed by the quality of the local Cabernets, they decided to buy property and start a winery in Creston. Michael believes Chateau Margene's location is ideal: "The Templeton Gap influence offers cool nightly breezes after hot summer days, the perfect scenario for growing Cabernet Sauvignon grapes."

The Mooneys' six-acre, low-yield vineyard grows the Cabernet Sauvignon, Cabernet Franc, and Merlot grapes that make up part of the winery's award-winning blends. "Great wine starts with great fruit," Michael explains. "To maintain a low-yield crop and increase fruit quality, we pay special attention to crop thinning, leaf removal, and regulated deficit irrigation." Chateau Margene also sources high-quality, low-yield fruit from three other vineyards in the Paso Robles appellation.

As a winemaker, Michael uses the Old World, French-style technique, taking extra precautions to avoid excessive handling and processing that can bruise the fruit. After the grapes are picked and brought into the winery, they are hand-sorted prior to de-stemming and left mostly whole when they're placed into the small, open-top fermentation bins. In most lots, the native yeast is allowed to remain and the juice is aged *sur lie* for about 18 months. French oak barrels are used almost exclusively to age all Chateau Margene wines; Chardonnay is aged for 6 to 12 months, and red wines for 30. Extreme care is taken to avoid all unnecessary movement of the wine, and vintages are allowed to contact stainless steel only prior to the bottling process.

Michael's gentle handling of his wines has proven a success: Chateau Margene's 2000 Cabernet Sauvignon took first place at the 2003 World Wine Market Cabernet Shootout—a blind tasting of more than 300 wines from all over the world. Chateau Margene wine is sold mainly at the winery and through the wine club.

Chateau Margene
4385 La Panza Road
Creston, CA 93432
(805) 238-2321
margenecel@aol.com
www.chateaumargene.com

Sub-AVA: Paso Robles

Owners:
Michael and Margene Mooney

Tasting Hours:
Noon – 6 p.m. Saturday – Sunday
(3rd Weekend March – Nov. 1)
And by appointment

Wines: Cabernet Sauvignon, Chardonnay, Zinfandel, Syrah, Sangiovese, Pinot Noir

Winemaker's Specialty:
Cabernet Sauvignon

Winemaker: Michael Mooney

Marinated Lamb Kabobs

1/2 c. Chateau Margene Cabernet Sauvignon
1/3 c. chicken broth
2 Tbsp. red wine vinegar
2 tsp. dried rosemary leaves, crushed
1 bay leaf
1 tsp. marjoram leaves, crushed
3 cloves garlic, minced
1 tsp. ginger root, finely chopped
1 tsp. salt
1-1/2 lbs. lamb sirloin roast, well trimmed and
  cut into 1-1/2-inch cubes

1 onion, cut into 1-1/2-inch pieces
1 red or yellow bell-pepper, cut into 1-1/2-inch pieces
4 wooden skewers, soaked in water

In a bowl, blend wine, broth, vinegar, herbs, garlic, ginger root, and salt. Add lamb cubes, cover, and refrigerate several hours or overnight. Skewer the lamb, onion, and bell pepper. Discard marinade. Grill over medium-hot coals for 5 minutes per side or for desired degree of doneness. Cover and let sit for 5 minutes. Enjoy with **Chateau Margene Cabernet Sauvignon.**

(Photo by Bill Charlesworth)

CHUMEIA VINEYARDS

Chumeia Vineyards takes its name from the ancient Greek word for "alchemy." In the Middle Ages, alchemists used a combination of chemistry and magic in an attempt to turn common metals into gold. At Chumeia Vineyards, the owners believe grape growing and winemaking are related to alchemy: "We take grapes, which are abundant, and through our winemaking process we turn then into something rare and precious." But the comparison with medieval science goes only so far—at Chumeia Vineyards, the grapes must be of a special quality to produce special wines, so that one kind of "gold" can be turned into another.

Chumeia Vineyards was founded in 2000 by four partners whose families had been in farming for more than 20 years: Lee Nesbitt; his father, Mark Nesbitt; John Simpson; and Eric Danninger. The four were already well acquainted with the hardships of farming —the long hours, unpredictable weather, the threats posed by insects— when they joined forces in their viticulture venture, but they claim it was their "youthful enthusiasm" that helped lay the groundwork for their winery. Lee, who learned the wine business during his years at J. Lohr and Meridian vineyards, acknowledges that being in the wine industry is a daunting task. "It takes a lot of work, drive, and motivation," he says.

The Chumeia Vineyards team believes the "alchemy" of producing special wine begins in the vineyard, where the grapevines absorb water and nutrients from the soil to produce Chumeia's "precious commodity"— grapes. "You don't have to wave a magic wand or do anything special," says Lee. "You just need to put the right vine in the right soil and let nature take its course."

Lee, who is also Chumeia's winemaker, knows that great wine can't be made from mediocre fruit, because the grape lays the foundation for the wine. With a focus on producing "user-friendly, approachable wine," Chumeia Vineyards sources grapes from vineyards as far away as Monterey and the San Joaquin Valley. "All the flavors are in the soil," Lee adds. "We put the vineyard in the bottle, and the end result is better than gold."

Chumeia Vineyards
8331 Highway 46 East
Paso Robles, CA 93446
(805) 226-0102
lnesbitt@chumeiavineyards.com
www.chumeiavineyards.com

Sub-AVA: Paso Robles

Owners:
Lee Nesbitt, Mark Nesbitt,
John Simpson, Eric Danninger

Tasting Hours:
10 a.m. – 5 p.m. daily

Wines: Viognier, Pinot Noir, Cabernet Sauvignon, Zinfandel, Syrah

Winemaker's Specialties:
Viognier, Zinfandel

Winemaker: Lee Nesbitt

Calypso Grilled Jerk Hamburgers with Mango Salsa

2 Tbsp. jerk seasoning (*recipe below*)
1 lb. ground beef
4 sesame seed hamburger buns, toasted
1/4 c. mango salsa (*recipe right*)

Jerk Seasoning
1 Tbsp. each onion flakes, onion powder, ground thyme
2 tsp. salt
1 tsp. each cayenne, allspice, coarse-ground black pepper
1/4 tsp. each nutmeg, cinnamon
2 tsp. each sugar, dried chives, or green onions, minced
Mix together all ingredients. (Makes 3 tablespoons.)

Mango Salsa
1 c. very ripe mango, diced
2 Tbsp. red onion, minced
1 Tbsp. fresh cilantro, chopped
1 Tbsp. lime juice
Mix together all ingredients. (Makes 1-1/4 cups.)

Thoroughly mix ground beef and jerk seasoning in a large bowl. Shape into four patties. Grill patties until done. Place a burger on bottom half of each bun, top with mango salsa and top half of bun. Serve with sweet-potato chips and **Chumeia Syrah**.

WINE TASTING
Open Daily
10 AM to 5 PM

(Photo by Bill Charlesworth)

DARK STAR CELLARS

Dark Star Cellars focuses on the production of handcrafted "stellar" red wines, what vintner Norm Benson calls "dark stars of exceptional quality." Norm, who owns the small winery with his wife, Susan, and son, Brian, says it's up to them alone to create Dark Star Cellars' award-winning vintages.

"When we say we're a small family winery, we really mean it," Norm says. "It's just the three of us, so if we don't do the work, the work doesn't get done. Every wine that comes out of our winery has our fingerprints on the bottle."

Norm is the winemaker and attributes Dark Star Cellars' quality to the careful handling and personal supervision the wines receive from harvest to bottling, which allows each vintage to reach its full potential. All wine is moved gently from one area of the production facility to another by using low-pressure pneumatic pumps and nitrogen racking, a process Norm calls "synthetic gravity."

The winery is a place where the Bensons work together, producing wine and continuing a legacy of close family ties. The Dark Star label not only represents the Bensons' stellar red wine but also commemorates all the Benson family, especially Norm's father, Robert Phillip, who passed away in 1985.

Above the Dark Star logo, a triangular-shaped motif displays the words "Angeli d'Altri Tempi"—in Italian, "Angels from Other Times." The motto signals an awareness of the past, the present, and the future, and pays homage to Robert and the many people who have made positive contributions to the lives of Norm and his family.

Dark Star Cellars' special Bordeaux-style blend, "Ricordati"—Italian for "Always Remember"— also began as a tribute to Norm's father and memorializes all the Bensons' loved ones. Ricordati is 75 percent Cabernet Sauvignon, 15 percent Merlot, and 10 percent Cabernet Franc, and in wine competitions all over the world has won numerous gold medals and a Best of Class.

Dark Star Cellars
2985 Anderson Road
Paso Robles, CA 93446
(805) 237-2389
norm@darkstarcellars.com
www.darkstarcellars.com

Sub-AVA: Paso Robles

Owners: The Benson family

Tasting Hours:
11 a.m. – 5:30 p.m. Friday – Sunday

Wines: Merlot, Zinfandel, Bordeaux-style blends of Cabernet Sauvignon, Syrah

Winemaker's Specialties: Ricordati, Cabernet Sauvignon, Merlot

Winemaker: Norm Benson

Chanterelle Mushroom Salad with Roasted Garlic and Red Pepper Vinaigrette

1-1/2 c. wild chanterelle mushrooms
1 c. olive oil
1/4 c. roasted garlic
1/4 c. roasted red peppers
1/2 c. cider vinegar
1 tsp. salt
1 tsp. freshly ground pepper
2 oz. pea tendrils

Sauté mushrooms in 1 tsp. olive oil until tender. Set aside. Place garlic, peppers, and vinegar in blender and blend for 1 minute.

Add salt and pepper. While blending on medium speed, slowly add remaining olive oil until completely mixed. Toss pea tendrils in just enough vinaigrette to lightly coat (there will be some left over). Place on plate and top with mushrooms. (Note: Chanterelles are best in summer and winter.) Serve with **Dark Star Cellars Cabernet Sauvignon**.
Recipe courtesy Chef Matt G. Brehm, Mission Grill, San Luis Obispo

DOCE ROBLES WINERY & VINEYARD

Like many local vintners, Jim and Maribeth Jacobsen discovered the Paso Robles area during a 1990s wine-tasting trip. The Jacobsens recall, "We became hooked on the red-wine varietals and realized the potential for growing premium grapes that would translate into great wines." In 1997, they purchased 40 acres of rolling hills with an oak-crowned knoll on Twelve Oaks Drive. They named their winery Doce Robles—in Spanish "Twelve Oaks"—for the trees that grow on their property.

Third-generation grape growers from the San Joaquin Valley, Jim and Maribeth prefer red wine and planted their estate vineyard with red-grape varietals—Syrah, Zinfandel, Cabernet Sauvignon, Merlot, and Barbera. Since their first harvest in 1998, the Jacobsens have won numerous awards for their winemaking, including a gold medal at the 2002 Orange County Fair for their 1998 Robles Rojos red-wine blend; a double gold medal at the 2002 California State Fair for their 1999 Merlot; and a silver medal at the 2003 Jerry Mead New World Wine Competition for their 2000 Syrah.

Doce Robles' label is a reproduction of a painting by Fresno artist Gail Hansen, Maribeth's mother. Hansen's original oil of the winery's vineyard and oak trees is displayed on the tasting room wall. Indeed, the winery has an ambience of family and welcome. Visitors can usually find Jim and Maribeth behind the tasting bar, serving wine and chatting with guests, while Cruz, their Norwegian forest cat, naps in a basket at the end of the counter. The Jacobsens' five docile and friendly German shepherds—two are named Syrah and Zinny—often sleep in the driveway, unconcerned by guests arriving to sample the Jacobsens' award-winning red wines.

Doce Robles Winery & Vineyard
2023 Twelve Oaks Drive
Paso Robles, CA 93446
(805) 227-4766
docerobleswinery@tcsn.net
www.docerobles.com

Sub-AVA: Paso Robles

Owners:
Jim and Maribeth Jacobsen

Tasting Hours:
10 a.m. – 5:30 p.m. daily

Wines: Cabernet Sauvignon, Syrah, Zinfandel, Merlot, Barbera, Cabernet Franc, Chardonnay

Winemaker's Specialties:
Meritage blend, Cabernet Sauvignon, Merlot

Winemaker: Jim Jacobsen

Lamb Shanks with Syrah and Herbs

6 lamb shanks, preferably small in size
1 15-oz. can tomato sauce
1/4 c. Doce Robles Syrah
2 Tbsp. soy sauce
1 bay leaf
1/4 tsp. each marjoram and thyme
1/2 tsp. salt
1 clove garlic, sliced

Place shanks in a roasting pan with lid. Mix together remaining ingredients and pour over shanks. Cover and bake at 350° for 2 hours or until tender. Serve with **Doce Robles Syrah**.

DOVER CANYON WINERY

Named for the nearby forested canyon in northwest Paso Robles, Dover Canyon Winery specializes in extremely small quantities of vineyard-specific Syrah, Zinfandel, and Viognier wines. Owners Dan Panico and Mary Baker source the grapes for most of their artisan-style wines from specific microclimates within the northwest quadrant of the Paso Robles sub-AVA, where a strip of pre-calcareous shale runs through the region. "The high elevations, hilly terrain, and cool ocean breezes produce small, intensely flavored fruit with thick skins and dark pigments," says Dan, winemaker at Dover Canyon. "These grapes are optimal for Zinfandel and Rhône-style wines." Dover Canyon also supplies fruit from its own seven-acre, dry-farmed Zinfandel and Syrah estate vineyards.

"Our vintages reflect the vineyard, with a crisp acidity that offers longevity of fruit," says Dan. "My wines are robust, with distinctive smoke and licorice flavors and gentle perfumes of oak that don't overwhelm the fruit."

Dover Canyon Winery sits on a hilltop with a magnificent view of rolling ranch land and oak forests. As part of the National Wildlife Federation's worldwide network of "mini refuges," the winery provides a habitat for red-tailed hawks, wild turkeys, deer, badgers, bobcats, and other animals. Deer and raccoons frequently visit the winery's front lawn when they come to eat fruit from the nearby apple and nut trees.

Reflecting Dan and Mary's interest in animals, Dover Canyon's wine label is adorned with a reproduction of an artist's portrait of "Blue," a remarkable white Saint Bernard. (Dan and Mary invite Dover Canyon aficionados to read the saga of Blue on their Web site.) The label on the back of the bottle offers specific information about each wine: the name of the vineyard where the grapes were grown, the winemaking style employed, and the number of barrels made.

Dover Canyon Winery
4520 Vineyard Drive
Paso Robles, CA 93446
(805) 237-0101
dovercanyon@tcsn.net
www.dovercanyon.com

Sub-AVA: Paso Robles

Owners:
Dan Panico and Mary Baker

Tasting Hours:
11 a.m. – 5 p.m. Friday – Sunday

Wines:
Syrah, Zinfandel, and Viognier

Winemaker: Dan Panico

Grilled Mahi Mahi with Yogurt Tartar

2 mahi mahi steaks, about 1 inch thick
Juice of 1 navel orange
3 Tbsp. honey, slightly warmed
3 Tbsp. Mongolian Fire Oil (or any high-quality chili oil)
2 handfuls of fresh sage leaves, chopped fine
Black peppercorns, coarsely ground in a hand or coffee grinder
1 c. unflavored, live-culture yogurt
1/2 English or Armenian cucumber, peeled and chopped
1 Tbsp. fresh mint, chopped
1 Tbsp. fresh chives, chopped
Sea salt and black pepper to taste

Combine orange juice, honey, and chili oil in a small bowl; whisk thoroughly. Rub fish with chopped sage and freshly ground pepper. Place fish on medium-hot grill and baste with marinade. Grill for about 10 minutes until done, turning frequently with a large spatula and sprinkling with additional pepper. Mix together yogurt, cucumber, mint, chives, salt, and pepper and serve with fish and **Dover Canyon Zinfandel**.

DUNNING VINEYARDS

The trip to Dunning Vineyards is a scenic drive through the secluded hills of west Paso Robles. Dunning's 80-acre property has been in the Dunning family since 1960, when the historic homestead was purchased from the original owners. In 1991, Robert and Jo-Ann Dunning, along with Robert's siblings John Dunning and Barbara Dunning, founded Dunning Vineyards, where they planted their vineyard and began producing limited quantities of handcrafted, artisan estate wine.

"The 1,400-foot elevation and the calcareous-rock soil create ideal growing conditions for the low-yield vines that produce our Cabernet Sauvignon, Zinfandel, Merlot, and Chardonnay wines," says Robert. "The afternoon cooling effect of the Pacific Ocean extends the growing season and makes the fruit concentration more intense."

Robert's traditional winemaking practices include small-lot fermentation, gentle hand-punching of red wines, and barrel fermentation of white wines in 100 percent French oak barrels. These techniques result in wines that Robert believes are "incredibly rich, concentrated, and elegant."

The small, family-owned winery invites aficionados for "a dawn-to-dusk education" in winemaking and to observe the seasonal tasks at a working vineyard. The two-story Dunning Vineyard Country Inn, which opened in 2002, offers two comfortable guest suites in the completely renovated, circa-1920s homestead house that is pictured on the Dunning Vineyards wine label.

An overnight stay at the Country Inn includes a continental breakfast, a personal tour of the winery, and a private tasting at the Summer House tasting room, whose terrace overlooks the vineyards and provides a large, shaded picnic area. The inn's wraparound porch and an upstairs deck overlook the Merlot vineyard and a vista of century-old oak and pine trees, and are the perfect places to savor a bottle of Dunning's estate wine. Guests may also enjoy the optional, personal-chef services that feature seasonal, custom cuisine prepared in the guest-suite kitchens. A fireplace in the downstairs suite and a hydro-spa tub in the upstairs suite add to the enjoyment of this complete winery experience.

Dunning Vineyards
1953 Niderer Road
Paso Robles, CA 93446
(805) 238-4763
info@dunningwines.com
www.dunningvineyards.com

Sub-AVA: Paso Robles

Owners: Robert and Jo-Ann Dunning, John Dunning, Barbara Dunning

Tasting Hours:
11 a.m. – 5 p.m. Friday – Sunday
And weekdays by appointment

Wines: Cabernet Sauvignon, Zinfandel, Syrah, Merlot, Chardonnay

Winemaker's Specialty: Cabernet Sauvignon

Winemaker: Robert Dunning

Olive Tapenade and Goat Cheese Crostini

1 can black olives
3 to 4 cloves garlic, minced
2 Tbsp. Italian parsley, chopped
6 Tbsp. olive oil
1 baguette, sliced
Salt and pepper
1 log goat cheese

In a food processor, purée olives, garlic, and parsley. Drizzle in 2 to 3 Tbsp. olive oil to combine. Brush bread slices with remaining olive oil and season with salt and pepper. Place on a cookie sheet and toast in a 300° oven until browned. Spread goat cheese on crostini and spread with tapenade. Serve with **Dunning Vineyards Cabernet Sauvignon**.
Recipe courtesy Michele Ward, personal chef services, Dunning Vineyards

(*Photo courtesy Dunning Vineyards*)

EAGLE CASTLE WINERY

"Eagles soar, flags fly, and tranquility reigns" runs the well-chosen motto of Eagle Castle Winery. Situated majestically on a hill in east Paso Robles, the winery is a Renaissance-style castle complete with battlements, imposing custom-made doors, and a portcullis—a chain-suspended grated gate—that "guards" the castle entrance.

Life-size suits of armor greet visitors at the hospitality center, where castle guests can enjoy an eagle's-eye view of the countryside while tasting the winery's current releases. In addition to the tasting room, gift shop, barrel and fermentation rooms, case-goods storage area, and crush pad, the castle houses an unusual and impressive special events facility. There, Renaissance and Celtic décor creates a romantic ambiance for winemaker dinners, cooking-and-pairing classes, seminars, art exhibits, music festivals, and private parties. Guided tours are available for guests to see the winery's day-to-day operations.

Eagle Castle owners and managers Gary and Mary Lou Stemper have been viticulturists in the Paso Robles sub-AVA for many years and have long revered the region's exceptional promise for grape growing and wine production. In 2000, they founded Eagle Castle Winery, L.L.C., with investors to showcase their estate-grown fruit and develop an international reputation for fine wine.

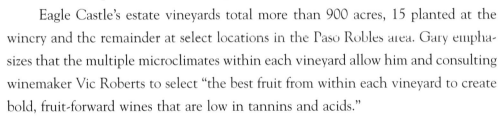

Eagle Castle's estate vineyards total more than 900 acres, 15 planted at the winery and the remainder at select locations in the Paso Robles area. Gary emphasizes that the multiple microclimates within each vineyard allow him and consulting winemaker Vic Roberts to select "the best fruit from within each vineyard to create bold, fruit-forward wines that are low in tannins and acids."

Eagle Castle's 2000 Cabernet Sauvignon won Best of Class at the 2003 California State Fair Wine Competition and a gold medal at the 2003 Los Angeles County Fair. Its 2001 Zinfandel received a gold medal at the 2004 Sacramento State Fair.

Eagle Castle Winery
3090 Anderson Way
Paso Robles, CA 93446
(805) 227-1428
gstemper@tcsn.net
www.eaglecastlewinery.com

Sub-AVA: Paso Robles

Owners: Gary and Mary Lou Stemper and Investors, L.L.C.

Tasting Hours:
10:30 a.m. – 5:30 p.m. daily

Wines: Chardonnay, Cabernet Sauvignon, Zinfandel, Viognier, Syrah Rosé, Syrah, Merlot, Royal Red blend, Late Harvest Zinfandel, Viognier

Winemakers' Specialties: Chardonnay, Cabernet Sauvignon, Zinfandel, Late Harvest Viognier

Winemakers: Gary Stemper, Vic Roberts (consultant)

Eagle Castle Beef Bourguignon

6 slices bacon
2 lbs. top sirloin, cut in bite-size pieces
1/4 c. flour
1 tsp. salt
1/4 tsp. pepper
1 10-oz. can beef consommé
1 c. Eagle Castle Cabernet Sauvignon
1 bay leaf
1 pint fresh mushrooms
2 c. carrots, sliced
1 16-oz. can whole onions, drained

Fry bacon in a skillet until crisp. Remove bacon, set aside, and leave drippings in the pan. Mix together flour, salt, and pepper, and add to pan with the beef. Cook until beef is browned. Stir in consommé, wine, and bay leaf. Cook uncovered until mixture boils. Cover, reduce heat, and simmer until tender. Remove bay leaf and cool. Add mushrooms, carrots, and onions, and simmer about 25 minutes, until vegetables are tender. Serve with French bread and **Eagle Castle Cabernet Sauvignon**.

(Photo courtesy Eberle Winery)

EBERLE WINERY

Thirty years ago, Gary Eberle had an epiphany that would one day result in Eberle Winery. After earning college degrees in biology and cellular genetics, Gary "stumbled upon the wonderful world of wine." Switching gears, he entered the University of California, Davis, doctoral winemaking program in 1973. After graduation, Gary managed his family's Paso Robles winery and in 1979 produced the first vintage of his own Eberle wine. Today, Gary is regarded as a Paso Robles grape-growing pioneer who specializes in wine made from grapes grown exclusively in the Paso Robles sub-AVA.

Eberle Winery is ranked among the 11 best wineries in California by *California Wine Winners 2004* (the ranking reflects a compilation of all the awards won in all wine competitions in a single year). Eberle also won the 2002 and 2003 *California Wine Winners* awards for best Viognier.

Eberle Winery's handsome tasting room is staffed with friendly, knowledgeable people who undergo a rigorous training program before they pour a glass of Eberle's prize-winning wines.

Outside the tasting room, the expansive Vineyard Deck is the perfect place to picnic and to enjoy the spectacular view of Eberle's estate vineyards and the dramatic sunsets above the coastal mountains. The covered, heated deck may also be reserved for a variety of private and special events ranging from elegant weddings to *al fresco* dinners and casual barbeques.

Eberle Winery is proud to offer fun and informative tours of its winemaking facility, which includes extensive wine caves. Under the winery, 16,000 square feet of rambling caves provide a naturally cool and high-humidity environment for the aging of Eberle's red wines. A series of winemaker dinners is offered to the public in the romantic ambience of the caves' Wild Boar Room, a formal dining room where educational wine seminars and corporate meetings and events can also be arranged.

Eberle Winery
3810 Highway 46 East
Paso Robles, CA 93446
(805) 238-9607
info@eberlewinery.com
www.eberlewinery.com

Sub-AVA: Paso Robles

Owner: Gary Eberle

Tasting Hours:
10 a.m. – 6 p.m. daily (Summer)
10 a.m. – 5 p.m. daily (Winter)

Wines: Cabernet Sauvignon, Viognier, Syrah, Syrah Rosé, Zinfandel, Chardonnay, dessert wines

Winemaker's Specialties: Cabernet Sauvignon, Viognier

Winemaker: Ben Mayo

Gary's Pasta Carbonara

1 lb. linguine or spaghetti pasta
4 gloves garlic, minced
3 eggs
2 oz. grated Parmesan cheese and 1 oz. grated Romano
1/2 tsp. each dried oregano and basil
1/4 tsp. red pepper flakes
1/4 c. olive oil
1/2 lb. thick bacon, cut into strips
1/2 c. white wine

Whisk garlic, eggs, cheese, herbs, and red pepper flakes in small bowl. Fry bacon in olive oil while pasta is boiling. When bacon is crisp, remove and add white wine to pan to deglaze. Put cooked pasta in bowl, toss in egg mixture. Add bacon and white-wine mixture. Serve immediately with bread, butter, and **Eberle Estate Cabernet Sauvignon**.

EOS ESTATE WINERY

Named for the Greek goddess of the dawn, EOS Estate Winery is one of the largest family-owned wineries in Paso Robles. Located on 700 acres of estate vineyards and gardens, the spectacular 104,000-square-foot, Romanesque-style facility is also a travel destination. Guests are invited to take an informative, self-guided tour, picnic on the artfully landscaped grounds, browse the impressive and well-stocked Mediterranean Marketplace gift shop and deli, and visit the race car exhibit, which is housed inside the tasting room.

EOS Estate Winery was founded in 1996 as a partnership among the Arciero family, the Underwood family, and Kerry Vix. Soon, the winery that specializes in Petite Sirah became one of California's fastest-growing wine brands. Since the first bottling in 1997, EOS has won numerous awards. Its 1997 Petite Sirah, Zinfandel, and Sauvignon Blanc each took Best of Class at the 1997 California State Fair Wine Competition. The 1999 EOS Reserve Petite Sirah received seven gold medals from prestigious worldwide competitions, and respected American wine critic Dan Berger rated it "exceptional." EOS has also been recognized and awarded for its innovative packaging, which includes an elegant, embossed pewter label on its 2000 Paso Robles Zinfandel Port.

The EOS portfolio includes the "Cupa Grandis" Grand Barrel Reserve label, which features wine made from the best blocks of grapes in the EOS estate Chardonnay and Petite Sirah vineyards. The Cupa Grandis Chardonnay is fermented and aged in new Louis-Latour French oak barrels, and the Petite Sirah in barrels made

from specific French forests chosen by winemaker Leslie Melendez. Leslie handcrafts all EOS wines with an emphasis on producing what she calls "food-friendly wines that are well balanced, elegant, and fruit forward."

EOS also produces two lines of more competitively priced wines under the "Novella" and "Arciero" labels. In 1999, EOS added a 24,000-square-foot barrel storage room to accommodate the growing number of barrels needed to age the winery's many vintages.

EOS Estate Winery
5625 Highway 46 East
Paso Robles, CA 93446
(805) 239-2562
info@eosvintage.com
www.eosvintage.com

Sub-AVA: Paso Robles

Owners: The Arciero family, the Underwood family, Kerry Vix

Tasting Hours:
10 a.m. – 5 p.m. daily
10 a.m. – 6 p.m. Fri. – Sat.
(Memorial Day through Labor Day)

Wines: Petite Sirah, Zinfandel, Cabernet Sauvignon, Merlot, Chardonnay, Sauvignon Blanc, dessert wines

Winemaker's Specialty: Petite Sirah

Winemaker: Leslie Melendez

Chris' Caribbean Beef Stew

1-1/2 lbs. stew beef
2 Tbsp. olive oil
1 14-oz. can each beef and chicken stock
3 c. water
1/4 c. soy sauce
Juice of 3 limes
1 c. each, sliced celery and carrots
2 c. diced new potatoes
2 chayote squash, diced
1 yellow onion, chopped
2 jalapeño or serrano peppers, minced

1 15-oz. can red or black beans, drained and rinsed
1 Tbsp. chopped ginger root
5 cloves garlic, crushed
1-1/2 Tbsp. allspice
2 Tbsp. fresh thyme, chopped
Black pepper to taste
Cilantro and parsley, chopped

Cut beef into 1-inch cubes. Brown in olive oil. Add remaining ingredients, bring to boil, and simmer for 4 hours. Serve over rice and garnish with chopped cilantro and parsley. Serve with **EOS Zinfandel**.

(Photos courtesy EOS Estate Winery)

GREY WOLF CELLARS

Grey wolves are social animals with a strong sense of family—the pack includes aunts and uncles as well as parents and offspring. When Joe and Shirlene Barton founded their winery, they named it Grey Wolf Cellars to symbolize the Bartons' spirit of family working together for a common goal.

In the1980s, Joe and Shirlene became acquainted with premium wines at their family-owned restaurant in Steamboat Springs, Colo. Shirlene recalls, "Joe and I often talked about someday making our own wine."

In the mid-1990s, the Bartons moved back to their native California and purchased farmland on Highway 46 West in Paso Robles. Joe and Shirlene converted an outbuilding into a winemaking facility and the property's 1949 farmhouse into a tasting room. They first planted two acres of vines—playfully named "The Big Bad Wolf Vineyard"—and added six more acres in the following years.

From the beginning, Joe wanted to make his new business venture a family affair. The first Grey Wolf wine labels read, "A family is a circle of caring, strong and eternal." In 1998, Joe passed away, but his legacy of winemaking lives on in son Joe Jr., who was well prepared to assume his father's duties as winemaker—Joe Jr. received a degree in fruit science from California Polytechnic State University in San Luis Obispo.

Grey Wolf's Old World-style winemaking technique aims at enhancing the grape's natural flavor: Joe Jr. believes that using small, open-top fermentation bins and hand punch-down helps bring out the fruit's true taste.

Some of Grey Wolf's varietals have lighthearted names like "Little Red," "Wolfpack," and "Puppy Love." All wines are adorned with labels that are reproductions of original paintings by nationally known Western artist Larry Bees of Paso Robles.

Grey Wolf Cellars
2174 Highway 46 West
Paso Robles, CA 93446
(805) 237-0771
greywolf@tcsn.com
www.grey-wolfcellars.com

Sub-AVA: Paso Robles

Owners:
Shirlene Barton, Joe Barton Jr.

Tasting Hours:
11 a.m.– 5:30 p.m. daily

Wines: Viognier, Roussanne, White Zinfandel, Grenache, Cabernet Sauvignon, Merlot, Syrah, Zinfandel, and red wine blends

Winemaker's Specialty:
Estate Zinfandel (Big Bad Wolf Vineyard)

Winemaker: Joe Barton Jr.

Korean BBQ Tri-Tip

2 to 4 lbs. tri-tip, trimmed of fat
1 c. soy sauce
1/4 c. sesame oil
1 c. white sugar
1/4 c. brown sugar
1/4 c. fresh garlic, minced
1/4 c. fresh ginger, minced
2 Tbsp. ground pepper
2 c. sesame seeds
2 c. green onion, chopped
1 c. Grey Wolf Zinfandel

In a large bowl, mix soy sauce, oil, and sugars until sugars are dissolved. Add garlic, ginger, pepper, and sesame seeds, and mix thoroughly. Add onion and 1/2 cup wine, stirring well. Marinate meat several hours or overnight. Sear meat for 10 minutes on a medium-hot grill, turning often. Continue grilling for 30 to 40 minutes, drizzling the remaining wine over meat to impart a wine-reduction flavor. Serve with **Grey Wolf Big Bad Vineyard Zinfandel.**

HARMONY CELLARS

Harmony Cellars is a mom-and-pop winery "dedicated to making superior wine that doesn't cost a king's ransom," according to Chuck Mulligan, who founded the winery with his wife, Kim, in 1989. Built on dairy farmland that has been in Kim's family for generations, the winery is a joint effort—Chuck is the winemaker and Kim is the business manager who runs day-to-day operations.

Chuck and Kim like "the European approach to wine" in which wine is customarily served at dinner, as an integral part of family life. Chuck's belief that "people need to loosen up a little about wine" inspired him to create handcrafted wines with "balance and flavor" that sold at reasonable prices, so people could enjoy them on a regular basis.

Harmony Cellars' nationally distributed wines are made on the premises and result from Chuck's winemaking philosophy: "Make wine to complement food and let the grape express its character." Chuck sources grapes primarily from the Paso Robles sub-AVA and Chardonnay grapes from the region's Templeton Gap area.

Harmony Cellars has received national acclaim for its wines: The 2001 Chardonnay took home the double gold medal at the 2003 Amenti del Vino Wine Competition, and the silver at the 2003 San Francisco Chronicle Wine Competition. The 2000 Syrah won the Best of Class gold at the 2003 West Coast Wine Competition. And the 2001 Diamond Reserve Chardonnay received the silver at the El Dorado County Fair Wine Competition and the bronze at the Indiana State Fair International Wine Competition.

Chuck and Kim built their rustic wood winery and tasting room to reflect the country atmosphere of the surrounding area. Standing on a bluff overlooking the pastoral artisans' town of Harmony, the tasting room and patio offer a remarkable view of the hamlet and hills just inland from the ocean. Harmony Cellars' gift shop is stocked with artistically displayed, unusual gift items and gourmet foods, including savory oils, decadent chocolates, a variety of mustards, and specialty wine accessories.

Harmony Cellars
3255 Harmony Valley Road
P. O. Box 2502
Harmony, CA 93435
(805) 927-1625
tastingroom@harmonycellars.com
www.harmonycellars.com

AVA: Central Coast

Owners: Chuck and Kim Mulligan

Tasting Hours:
10 a.m. – 5 p.m. daily

Wines: Chardonnay, Cabernet Sauvignon, Zinfandel, port

Winemaker's Specialty:
Chardonnay

Winemaker: Chuck Mulligan

Chuck's Port and Berry Compote

1/2 bottle Harmony Cellars Port (375 ml)
4 Tbsp. brown sugar
Dash each nutmeg and cinnamon
1-1/2 cup berries (strawberries, blueberries, raspberries, etc.)

Pour port into a small pan. Simmer, do not boil, until port is reduced by half. Stir in brown sugar, nutmeg, and cinnamon. Let cool and add berries. Let compote sit for at least one hour before serving with **Harmony Cellars Diamond Reserve Port.**

HUNT CELLARS

Since its founding, Hunt Cellars has consistently produced highly acclaimed vintages. The Paso Robles winery has won numerous gold medals and Best of Class citations at wine competitions, and has regularly received ratings of 90+ points from publications like *Wine Enthusiast* magazine. The American Wine Society, the Wine Council, and famed critic Robert Dierker have selected Hunt as the next "cult winery," a description that well describes the vision of David Hunt, winemaker and owner of Hunt Cellars.

A former musician and entrepreneur, David began his third career in 1996 when he and his wife, Debby, purchased 550 acres in Creston, overlooking the horse farm owned by "Jeopardy" television host Alex Trebec. With a variety of terrain and soil types and four distinct microclimates, the property offered exceptional potential for the cultivation of premium grapes. In the late 1990s, David took enology classes through the extension program at the University of California, Davis. In 1997, he released his first wine under the Hunt Cellars label.

Two years later, David and Debby opened the Hunt Cellars tasting room at Highway 46 West and Oakdale Road. The Hunts' friendly staff guides wine tasters in sampling the award-winning varietals Hunt Cellars has to offer, which are sold at select restaurants and wine shops. The tasting room's spacious deck overlooks a lush, green lawn and provides tables and a pleasant outdoor setting for picnics.

Among Hunt Cellars' many accolades are four gold medals and one Best of Class for its 2000 Cabernet Bon Vivant, four gold medals and two Best of Class for its 2001 Syrah Hilltop Serenade, and seven gold medals and three Best of Class for its 2001 Barbera Starving Artist Vineyards.

Though David has won hundreds of awards for his wines, he emphasizes, "My goal is to create memorable wines that become part of your life, the kind that prompt you to remember not only the wine but also the fabulous meal and the great company you enjoyed that evening."

Hunt Cellars
2875 Oakdale Road
Paso Robles, CA 93446
(805) 237-1600
huntcellars@huntcellars.com
www.huntwinecellars.com

Sub-AVA: Paso Robles

Owners: David and Debby Hunt

Tasting Hours:
10:30 a.m.– 6 p.m. daily (Summer)
10:30 a.m. – 5:30 p.m. daily (Winter)

Wines: Cabernet Sauvignon, Sangiovese, Syrah, Zinfandel, Barbera, Petit Syrah, red wine blends, Chardonnay, Sauvignon Blanc

Winemaker's Specialties: Cabernet Sauvignon, Zinfandel

Winemaker: David Hunt

Zinballs: Spicy Zinfandel Meatballs

1 Tbsp. olive oil
1 onion, chopped
8 cloves fresh garlic
1 each bell and jalapeño pepper
8 oz. barbeque sauce
1 c. each catsup and vinegar
Pinch of cumin
1/2 tsp. each red and Santa Fe pepper
2 Tbsp. brown sugar
2 to 3 lbs. homemade meatballs
1 c. Zinfandel
Freshly ground black pepper

In a large sauce pan sauté onion, garlic, and bell and jalapeño peppers in olive oil. Add barbeque sauce, catsup, vinegar, cumin, red pepper, Santa Fe dry pepper, and brown sugar. Mix well. Gently fold meatballs into sauce. Over medium-high heat, allow mixture to boil for 5 minutes. Reduce heat, add up to 1 cup Zinfandel, and simmer for 30 to 60 minutes. Garnish with freshly ground black pepper. Enjoy with **Hunt Cellars Old Vine Zinfandel** or **Outlaw Ridge Zinfandel**.

J. LOHR VINEYARDS & WINES

In the early 1970s, Central Coast viticulture pioneer Jerry Lohr planted his first vineyard in Monterey County, where he became renowned for his prize-winning, white-grape varietals, including the J. Lohr Estates Riverstone Chardonnay.

More than 10 years later, Jerry became interested in the then little-known wine-producing region of Paso Robles after tasting Cabernet Sauvignon made from fruit grown in the area. In 1986, Jerry purchased property on Airport Road in Paso Robles and planted Cabernet Sauvignon, Merlot, and other red-grape varieties. While Jerry cultivated his vines, he constructed adjacent to his vineyard a winery and barrel facility, and a tasting room with a large veranda that opened in 1988.

Today, Jerry considers J. Lohr Vineyards & Wines a "wine-growing" rather than a grape-growing enterprise, because he believes the essence of good wine begins in the vineyard. Paying more attention to the fruit's actual flavor than to its sugar level and acidity, Jerry often picks his grapes several weeks later than the conventional harvest time. "The result is greater flavor intensity before the grapes are even crushed," he explains.

"J. Lohr's goal," says Jerry, "is to produce varietals that can stand beside the best in the world." This ambitious goal led to the creation of three tiers of wine in the J. Lohr portfolio, each produced from its estate vineyards: the "Cuvée" series, limited in production and made only from grapes deemed exceptional; the J. Lohr "Vineyard" series, also limited in production and considered a luxury wine; and the J. Lohr "Estates," the winery's signature series, produced from its vineyards in Monterey County and Paso Robles.

Although operated as a boutique winery, J. Lohr enjoys the benefits of a cutting-edge laboratory and state-of-the-art winemaking equipment. These sophisticated technologies coupled with Jerry's expertise and the quality of J. Lohr's estate vineyards have created award-winning wines, including the 1999 Hilltop Paso Robles Cabernet Sauvignon, which won a double gold medal at the 2003 San Francisco International Wine Competition and a gold medal at the 2003 Florida State Fair, and was voted one of the 20 Most Popular Cabernets in *Wine & Spirit* magazine's 2003 Annual Restaurant Poll.

J. Lohr Vineyards & Wines
6169 Airport Road
Paso Robles, CA 93446
(805) 239-8900
info@jlohr.com
www.jlohr.com

Sub-AVA: Paso Robles

Owner: Jerry Lohr

Tasting Hours:
10 a.m. – 5 p.m. daily

Wines: Cabernet Sauvignon, Chardonnay

Winemaker's Specialties: Estates Seven Oaks Cabernet Sauvignon, Estates Riverstone Chardonnay

Winemaker: Jeff Meier

Braised Lamb Shanks with J. Lohr South Ridge Syrah Sauce

1 Tbsp. unsalted butter
2 Tbsp. olive oil
2 1-lb. lamb shanks, cut in half crosswise
Salt to taste
1 medium onion, finely chopped
1 16-oz. can peeled Italian tomatoes with liquid, chopped
6 cloves garlic, chopped
1 c. J. Lohr South Ridge Syrah
1 14-1/2-oz. can chicken stock
12 ea. parsley stems and juniper berries, crushed
7 thyme sprigs
1/3 c. Italian parsley, chopped

Melt butter and oil in a large cast-iron casserole dish. Season shanks with salt; add to casserole and brown on all sides. Remove to plate and pour off all but 1 Tbsp. fat. Cook onion in fat until golden brown. Add tomatoes and garlic and cook over high heat for 3 minutes. Add shanks, wine, stock, parsley, juniper berries, and thyme. Bring to a boil. Cover casserole and place in 350° oven. Bake for 30 minutes, turn shanks, and bake for 2-1/2 hours, adding more stock halfway through cooking time if necessary. Discard herb stems, stir in chopped parsley, and enjoy with the remaining **J. Lohr South Ridge Syrah.**

JUSTIN VINEYARDS & WINERY

For wine enthusiasts and gourmet diners intent on pairing food with the perfect wine, JUSTIN Vineyards & Winery in west Paso Robles is a trendsetter in guiding discriminating palates to the marriage of fine vintages and expertly prepared meals.

The winery's commitment to producing wines that complement and enhance world-class cuisine is embodied in JUSTIN's inn and French restaurant, where guests can savor the nuances of JUSTIN Vineyards' current releases while enjoying a truly elegant meal. Deborah's Room, the acclaimed four-star restaurant at the luxurious JUST Inn, offers an extraordinary dining experience.

"Our mission is to belong in the company of the finest wines in the world," say proprietors Justin and Deborah Baldwin. "Our wines are on the same restaurant wine lists and are sold to the same retailers as the finest Bordeaux blends."

Established in 1981, JUSTIN Vineyards & Winery produces handcrafted, internationally marketed estate wines. From its first vintages to its latest releases, JUSTIN has consistently received recognition for its quality. The 1994 ISOSCELES—a blend of Cabernet Sauvignon, Cabernet Franc, and Merlot—won the trophy for the best blended red wine in the world at the 2004 London International Wine & Spirit Competition's Pichon Longueville Comtesse de Lalande. In 2000, *Wine Spectator* magazine chose JUSTIN's 1997 vintage ISOSCELES as the "Sixth-Best Cabernet in the World."

In 2004, JUSTIN built the ISOSCELES Center "as a statement of grandeur and as a tribute to ISOSCELES, which has identified us as winemakers," explains Deborah. "The ISOSCELES Center is a culmination and representation of more than 20 years of hard work."

The facility encompasses 46,000 square feet and includes offices, an events room and a conference room, and wine caves that provide humidity-controlled storage as well as a venue for events, benefits, and conferences. JUSTIN Vineyards & Winery also offers monthly guest-chef dinners, featuring nationally acclaimed chefs who prepare special candlelit dinners served amid the barrels in the wine cellar.

JUSTIN Vineyards & Winery
11680 Chimney Rock Road
Paso Robles, CA 93446
(805) 238-6932
info@justinwine.com
www.justinwine.com

Sub-AVA: Paso Robles

Owners:
Justin and Deborah Baldwin

Tasting Hours:
10 a.m. – 6 p.m. daily

Wines: Bordeaux blends, Sauvignon Blanc, Chardonnay, Cabernet Sauvignon, Syrah, dessert wines

Winemaker's Specialty:
ISOSCELES Bordeaux blend

Winemaker: Fred Holloway

Pan-Roasted Venison with Morel Crust and Asparagus Purée

1 rack venison, bones and silver skin removed
1 bunch jumbo asparagus, peeled, with bottoms removed
2 Tbsp. butter
Salt and freshly ground black pepper to taste
2 oz. dried morel mushrooms
1 egg, well beaten
Flour for dredging
2 Tbsp. olive oil
Red-wine reduction sauce

Cook asparagus in boiling, salted water for 2 minutes. Place in a blender. Add butter, 4 Tbsp. of the cooking liquid, and salt and pepper, and purée until smooth. Keep warm. Coarsely grind mushrooms in a spice grinder, place on a plate, and set aside. Season venison with salt and pepper, dredge in flour, dip in egg, and then dredge in ground mushrooms. Heat oil in a sauté pan and sear venison on all sides. Place the pan in a 450° oven and bake for 7 to 10 minutes. Let venison rest for 2 minutes, then slice. Place a dollop of asparagus purée on a plate, top with two venison slices, and drizzle with red-wine reduction sauce. Serve with **JUSTIN Vineyards & Winery ISOSCELES**.
Recipe courtesy Chef Ryan Swarthout, Deborah's Room, Paso Robles

L'AVENTURE WINERY

Hidden at the end of a rugged road in the west hills of Paso Robles, L'Aventure Winery is hardly a secret—its Bordeaux-Rhône varietal blends have inspired a cult following among discriminating wine lovers. The 2002 *Los Angeles Times Magazine Annual Restaurant Issue* hailed veteran Bordeaux winemaker Stephan Asseo as a "renegade" for his "French varietals that may just put Paso Robles on the international map."

Born in Paris, Stephan graduated from enology college in Burgundy in the early 1980s and began to make wine from grapes grown on his family's three vineyards. Stephan soon earned critical acclaim and yearly accolades from the European press, international travel guides, and *Wine Spectator* magazine.

By the 1990s, Stephan wanted to expand his expertise and gain more freedom in viticulture and winemaking than the strict French appellation regulations would allow. A 1998 trip to California and its Central Coast was the beginning of L'Aventure—in French, "The Adventure." The quality of the westside Paso Robles *terroir* and climate convinced Stephan to buy 127 acres on Live Oak Road. From the first, Stephan had a well-defined winemaking goal: "I wanted to establish a winery in Paso Robles, to make a blend that expressed the area's varietals, quality, character, and *terroir*—not to make a copy of a Bordeaux blend."

Stephan's blending of Syrah and Cabernet Sauvignon has resulted in award-winning wines that he describes as "rich, concentrated, and intense, and a direct result of L'Aventure's high-density planting system." L'Aventure's vineyard contains 2,100 vines per acre, three times the number usually grown in similar California fields. "The dense planting produces a self-regulation of the vines," explains Stephan. "They compete for nutrients and therefore produce a lower yield, about one bottle per vine."

An award-winning winemaker in Europe, Stephan has received critical acclaim in the United States for his blends and single-vineyard wines. The August 2004 *Wine Advocate* magazine gave 94 points to his 2002 Estate Cuvée Paso Robles, 2002 Syrah Estate, and 2002 Cuvée Côte á Côte. In 2003, *Food & Wine* magazine rated L'Aventure a 98 for its overall production of Bordeaux- and Rhône-style blends.

L'Aventure Winery
2815 Live Oak Road
Paso Robles, CA 93446
(805) 227-1588
info@aventurewine.com
www.aventurewine.com

Sub-AVA: Paso Robles

Owner: Stephan Asseo

Tasting Hours:
11 a.m. – 4 p.m. Friday – Sunday
And by appointment

Wines: Paso Robles red wine blends, Roussanne, Syrah, Cabernet Sauvignon, Zinfandel

Winemaker's Specialty: "Paso Robles blend" of Cabernet Sauvignon and Syrah

Winemaker: Stephan Asseo

Roasted Squab with Red Wine Vinegar and Honey Sauce and Potato Gallette

6 small squabs
1/2 lb. butter
4 oz. onion, chopped
Fresh rosemary and thyme to taste
2 Tbsp. honey
1 c. red wine vinegar
1-1/2 c. chicken stock
2 lbs. potatoes, peeled and julienned
Salt and pepper to taste

Debone squabs, reserve bones, and set meat aside. Chop bones into small pieces and sauté with butter, onion, rosemary, and thyme. Brown well. Add honey and caramelize. Add vinegar and reduce sauce completely. Add stock and reduce sauce by half. Strain sauce, set aside, and discard bones. Place potatoes in a skillet, add salt, and cook until golden brown and crispy. Drain on a paper towel. Roast squabs in a 425° oven until breasts are medium rare, about 7 to 8 minutes. Finish the sauce by adding salt and pepper if needed and a little bit of butter. To serve, place potatoes and squabs side by side in the middle of a plate and pour the sauce around it. Garnish with fresh rosemary. Serve with **L'Aventure Optimus** or **Syrah**.
Recipe courtesy Chef Laurent Grangien, Bistro Laurent, Paso Robles

LE CUVIER WINERY

Le Cuvier Winery was established with the aim of remaining a small winery that produces fewer than 3,000 cases of wine each year.

Winery owners and partners John Munch and Mary Fox create limited lots of Cabernet Sauvignon, Zinfandel, Sangiovese, Syrah, Rhône blends, and Chardonnay that are available only at their tasting room and through their Elliptical Society Wine Club.

John began his winemaking career in 1981 when he founded Adelaida Cellars and became its winemaker. When Adelaida became a partnership and grew in size and production capacity, John left to pursue his dream of operating a small winery. He founded Le Cuvier in the west hills of Paso Robles in 1998, and later Mary Fox became his partner.

To purchase grapes for their limited lots of wine, John and Mary have longstanding contracts with chosen local vineyards.

"We only do business with 'limestone-soil vineyards,'" John explains, "because that soil grows the best grapes." His special relationship with area growers gives John complete control over all vineyard practices on land where grapes for his wines are grown and allows him to insist on the use of sustainable farming techniques.

John is also particular in his winemaking techniques. He adds no sulfites to the wine for at least two years, so the naturally occurring microflora and microfauna from the vineyard take part in the winemaking process.

"The result is a wine with a much broader spectrum of flavors, but a wine that takes longer to age and mature," says John, who emphasizes, "There's no substitute for time." Most Le Cuvier Chardonnay is aged for at least three years. Red wines are aged from three to five years, in neutral oak barrels that don't mask or interfere with the flavor of the grapes.

Le Cuvier Winery
9750 Adelaida Road
Paso Robles, CA 93446
(805) 238-5706
(800) 549-4764 toll free
contact@lcwine.com
www.lcwine.com

Sub-AVA: Paso Robles

Owners:
John Munch, Mary Fox

Tasting Hours:
11 a.m. – 5 p.m. daily

Wines: Cabernet Sauvignon, Zinfandel, Sangiovese, Syrah, Chardonnay, Rhône blends

Winemaker's Specialty:
Cabernet Sauvignon

Winemaker: John Munch

Blue Cheese Puffs

Cream puff pastry (per recipe)
Paprika
1/4 to 1/2 lb. blue cheese, Roquefort, or
  Gorgonzola (at room temperature)
10 oz. cream cheese, butter, or a combination
  of both (at room temperature)

Prepare cream puff dough according to recipe. Using a pastry bag with a round, 5/8-inch or star tip, pipe mixture in 1-inch diameters onto 2 parchment-lined baking pans. Sprinkle with paprika. Bake at 425° for 15 minutes. Rotate pans, reduce heat to 300°, and bake approximately 20 minutes longer or until golden brown and "lightweight." Remove from oven. With a toothpick or skewer, poke a hole in the side of each puff to release the air and create an opening for piping in the cheese mixture. In a food processor, blend together 3 parts blue, Roquefort, or Gorgonzola cheese to 1 part cream cheese and/or butter (to yield about 2 cups) until smooth and creamy. Using a medium, round tip, pipe mixture into puffs. Place filled puffs on a baking sheet in a 375° oven and heat for 2 to 3 minutes, until they "hiss" or slightly bubble. (Note: When using Gorgonzola, the cream cheese can be replaced with unsweetened Mascarpone and a dash of sage. Puffs can be filled ahead of time and refrigerated.) Serve with **Le Cuvier Cabernet Sauvignon**.

MALOY O'NEILL VINEYARDS

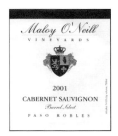

At Maloy O'Neill Vineyards, experimentation is a hallmark, a key part of the process in creating small lots of site-specific, handcrafted wines.

"I'm always looking for ways to improve the vineyard and my winemaking techniques, and to raise the bar for the entire Paso Robles region," says winery owner and winemaker Shannon O'Neill. "Only after many years do you start to figure out what works and what doesn't."

Maloy O'Neill Vineyards is not a newcomer to the wine business. Since 1982, the vineyard has been growing grapes for many wineries in the Paso Robles area, and for wineries in Napa, Sonoma, Mendocino, and Lake counties. In 2000, Shannon and his wife, Maureen, began producing their own wine under the Maloy O'Neill Vineyards label to gain recognition for their grapes. Soon their venture grew into a full-scale winemaking operation.

To increase the varietal character of Maloy O'Neill wine, Shannon uses a variety of grape clones for each vintage, experiments with farming and production techniques, uses numerous canopy-management and leaf- and cluster-thinning styles, and tries various cold-soak and fermentation processes.

Shannon is a specialist in fermentation and the chemistry aspects of winemaking. He earned a degree in fermentation science at the University of California, Davis, honing his skills as he worked at wineries and as an intern in the chemistry labs of several large companies. After graduation, Shannon went on to become an industrial-fermentation researcher for a biotechnology company in the Silicon Valley.

Shannon's years of education, research, and winemaking and vineyard experimentation have earned Maloy O'Neill Vineyards numerous accolades. The 2004 West Coast Wine Competition awarded gold medals to the 2002 Gioi blend and the 2002 Cabernet Sauvignon, and a silver medal to the 2002 Private Reserve Syrah. At the 2004 Los Angeles County Fair Wine Competition, Maloy O'Neill's 2002 Merlot won the silver medal, and its 2002 Syrah, Windy Hill, Paso Robles, received the bronze.

Maloy O'Neill Vineyards
5725 Union Rd.
Paso Robles, CA 93446
(805) 238-7320
winery@maloyoneill.com
www.maloyoneill.com

Sub-AVA: Paso Robles

Owners:
Shannon and Maureen O'Neill

Tasting Hours:
Noon - 5 p.m. daily

Wines: Cabernet Sauvignon, Syrah, Zinfandel, Merlot, Pinot Noir, blends

Winemaker's Specialties:
Cabernet Sauvignon, Syrah

Winemaker: Shannon O'Neill

Stuffed Leg of Lamb

1 3- to 4-lb. leg of lamb, boned and butterflied
2 links sweet Italian sausage
1 large onion, finely chopped
2 cloves garlic, minced
1 large stalk celery, finely chopped
1 pkg. frozen chopped spinach
1/2 8-oz. can water chestnuts, coarsely chopped
1/8 lb. white pistachio nuts
3 Tbsp. Romano cheese, grated
2 eggs, beaten
2 slices slightly stale bread, cubed
Pinch of sage
Salt and pepper to taste

Sauté sausage, remove from pan, and coarsely chop. Add onion, garlic, and celery to pan and sauté in fat until soft. Cook spinach according to package directions and drain well. In a large bowl mix sausage, cooked vegetables, and all remaining ingredients. Lay meat on a flat surface and fill with stuffing. Roll up meat beginning at the smallest end and tie well. Bake on rack at 375° until meat thermometer registers medium rare. Serve with gravy or mint jelly and **Maloy O'Neill Syrah.**

MARTIN & WEYRICH
WINERY & TASTING ROOM

At Martin & Weyrich Winery & Tasting Room, Italy is the theme in the Tuscan-style tasting room with yellow stucco walls and a red-tiled roof that stands prominently at the corner of Highway 46 East and Buena Vista Drive. A major producer of Cal-Italia wines, Martin & Weyrich is dedicated to "uncovering the age-old secrets of Italian varietals."

The winery was founded as Martin Brothers Winery in 1981 by siblings Tom, Nick, Mary, and Ann Martin, the children of Edward T. Martin, a marketing manager of a wine distribution company and the editor of a wine trade magazine. Situated on 83 acres of former dairy land, Martin Brothers was one of the first contemporary wineries in America to grow and produce Nebbiolo (the principal grape variety of the Piedmont region of northwest Italy) and Sangiovese.

In 1998, David and Mary Martin Weyrich and their children became the sole owners of the nearly 20-year-old winery, changing its name to Martin & Weyrich Winery & Tasting Room. Today, the Weyrich family is working to further enhance the winery's reputation as a major producer of Italian varietals.

Martin & Weyrich produces two versions of Nebbiolo, including their Reserve Nebbiolo Vecchio, which is made from the vineyard's highest quality grapes and aged for more than two years in new French oak barrels. "Nebbiolo gives you the power and structure of Cabernet and the perfume and elegance of Pinot Noir," says David. "It's excellent with game and roasted meats." Martin & Weyrich also produces white-wine varietals, including Pinot Grigio and Chardonnay, from its 100-acre estate vineyard in the Edna Valley.

Martin & Weyrich's luxurious Villa Toscana Bed and Breakfast provides an escape to a fantasy of Old Italy. The extraordinary stone "village" is nestled in Martin & Weyrich's estate vineyards and features a bistro-style restaurant, a private banquet room and kitchen for special events and weddings, exquisite guest suites, and in-room spa treatments.

**Martin & Weyrich Winery
& Tasting Room**
4230 Buena Vista Drive
Paso Robles, CA
(805) 238-2520
sales@martinweyrich.com
www.martinweyrich.com

Sub-AVA: Paso Robles

Owners: David and Mary Weyrich

Tasting Hours:
10 a.m. – 6 p.m. daily (Summer)
10 a.m. – 5 p.m. daily (Winter)

Wines: Muscato Allegra, Sangiovese, Nebbiolo, Zinfandel, Chardonnay, Pinot Grigio

Winemakers' Specialty: Nebbiolo

Winemakers:
Craig Reed, Alan Kinne

Crab Cakes Appetizer

1 lb. crabmeat
1/2 c. diced red bell pepper
1/2 c. diced onion
2 tsp. lemon juice
1 pinch each, salt and pepper
2 oz. mayonnaise
1/2 oz. Dijon mustard
Bread crumbs (Panko brand, found at Japanese markets) or seasoned crumbs

Mix all ingredients in a medium bowl. Form into cakes, drudge in crumbs, and sauté on medium until golden brown. Serve with **Martin & Weyrich Hidden Valley Chardonnay.**

MASTANTUONO WINERY

A fourth-generation winemaker whose ancestors came from Italy's Tufo region, Pasquale Mastantuono claims, "Winemaking is in my blood." Pasquale's winemaking days began in Detroit, when at age 12 he helped his two Italian grandfathers make hearty, robust red wines. He fondly remembers the family anxiously awaiting the arrival of Zinfandel grapes, which had made "the long journey" from California.

Pasquale later moved to Southern California and began a career as a manufacturer of custom furniture. In his spare time, he made wine at his Topanga Canyon home, where he often held blind wine tastings for friends, pouring high-priced wines along with his homemade varietals. "Quite often my homemade wines won out over many expensive vintages," admits the former amateur winemaker.

In 1976, Pasquale sold his furniture business to pursue his lifelong dream of devoting all his time to producing premium wines. He purchased 65 acres of oak-studded land in Paso Robles and planted 17 acres of Zinfandel vines. Pasquale says the planting of the vineyard began "a love affair" with Zinfandel, which ultimately earned him the nickname "Zinman." The attractive Mastantuono Winery tasting room designed and built by Pasquale in 1983 includes a residence where he lives with his wife, Karen, and their two children. Today, the tasting room is one of the busiest in the region, offering fine wines along with a variety of gourmet foods and unusual gifts.

In celebration of his European heritage, Pasquale now produces many Italian varietals, including Barbera, Sangiovese, and Nebbiolo. Mastantuono also bottles a wine from the Carmine grape, a varietal created at the University of California, Davis, by crossing Cabernet Sauvignon, Merlot, and Carignane. Pasquale says the wine will surprise tasters, as it's "on the heavy side and very distinctive." Zinfandel, however, remains Pasquale's favorite varietal, a wine that he insists is "the best in the world."

Mastantuono Winery
2720 Oak View Road
Templeton, CA 93465
(805) 238-0676
info@mastantuonowinery.com
www.mastantuonowinery.com

Sub-AVA: Paso Robles

Owner: Pasquale Mastantuono

Tasting Hours:
10 a.m. – 6 p.m. daily (Summer)
10 a.m. – 5 p.m. daily (Winter)

Wines: Zinfandel, Barbera, Cabernet Sauvignon, Carminello, Carmine, Sangiovese, Muscat Canelli, Nebbiolo, Chardonnay, Chenin Blanc, Pinot Grigio, White Zinfandel

Winemaker's Specialty: Zinfandel

Winemaker: Pasquale Mastantuono

Herb-Crusted Pork Tenderloin

2 lbs. pork tenderloin
2 Tbsp. each fresh rosemary, thyme, marjoram, sage, chopped
1/2 tsp. ground coriander
1/4 tsp. each salt and pepper
2 to 3 Tbsp. olive oil
3 cloves garlic, slivered

Cut 1-inch slits in meat. Mix together herbs, coriander, salt, pepper, and olive oil. Rub mixture onto meat and into slits. Insert garlic slivers into slits. Wrap and refrigerate 4 to 6 hours or overnight. Place meat in a shallow roasting pan, insert meat thermometer, and roast at 325° until meat thermometer registers 160°. Serve with **Mastantuono Zinfandel**.

MERIDIAN VINEYARDS

At Meridian Vineyards, winemaker Signe Zoller has won the reputation of an "appellation specialist." Signe received her master's degree in enology at the University of California, Davis, and intimately understands the individual nuances of the Meridian estate vineyards in Paso Robles, Edna Valley, and Santa Barbara County, and the five vineyards within the Central Coast AVA from which Meridian sources grapes. Signe has a passion for the art of winemaking, involving herself firsthand in every aspect of grape growing and wine production. Acclaimed for the winery's flagship Santa Barbara County Chardonnay, Signe carefully selects the grapes she will use for Meridian's single-vineyard vintages or blends.

Signe is also ardent about sharing her knowledge with others, so that everyone, especially women, will feel comfortable serving wine at home or ordering from a menu. She offers her expertise in two informative pamphlets, *Seven Things Every Woman Should Know About Serving Wine* and *Seven Things Every Gal Should Know About Ordering Wine*, both available at Meridian's tasting room. Signe's informed writings give advice on everything from entertaining and food-and-wine pairing to navigating a restaurant's wine list, but most importantly they encourage wine lovers to take pleasure in, and enjoy the experience of, tasting favorite and new vintages.

Surrounded by majestic, 200-year-old oak trees, Meridian's handsome, natural-stone tasting room and patio offer a commanding view of the winery's Home Vineyard and provide a memorable setting for private parties and weddings. The exceptionally attractive grounds, meandering paths, and fragrant herb garden comprising more than 200 varieties beckon visitors to stroll, relax, and picnic. Impromptu picnics are made easy by the assortment of cheeses and salamis found in the tasting room's deli case or by custom-made boxed lunches visitors can order by phone before arriving. Gourmet foods, glassware gift items, apparel, cookbooks, pottery, table linens, and baskets are also available in the sun-filled tasting room, where Meridian's staff prides itself in making wine tasting "unhurried and friendly."

Meridian Vineyards
7000 Highway 46 East
Paso Robles, CA 93446
(805) 226-7133
merwineclub@meridianvineyards.com
www.meridianvineyards.com

Sub-AVA: Paso Robles

Owner:
Beringer Blass Wine Estates

Tasting Hours:
10 a.m. – 5 p.m. daily

Wines: Chardonnay, Pinot Grigio, Sauvignon Blanc, Gewürztraminer, Pinot Noir, Merlot, Cabernet Sauvignon, Syrah/Shiraz

Winemaker's Specialty: Santa Barbara County Chardonnay

Winemaker: Signe Zoller

Pesto Cheese Crisps

7 7-inch flour tortillas
1 7-oz. container pesto sauce
3-1/2 c. shredded mozzarella cheese
28 sun-dried tomato halves (packed in oil), julienned

Preheat oven to 500°. Arrange tortillas on several large baking sheets. Spread 2 Tbsp. pesto over one side of each tortilla, about 1/2 inch from the edge, and top with 1/2 c. cheese and 1/7th of the tomatoes. Bake about 5 to 6 minutes, until cheese is bubbly and beginning to brown and tortillas are crisp and golden. Cut into 6 wedges and serve immediately with **Meridian Vineyards Merlot** or **Syrah**.

MIDNIGHT CELLARS

Some wine aficionados fantasize about transforming their lifestyles, of quitting their nine-to-five jobs and moving out of the city to open a winery. But how many wine lovers actually summon the resolve to make their dream a reality? Meet the Hartenberger family: Bob and Mary Jane, their sons, Mike and Rich, and Rich's wife, Michelle. In 1995, the Hartenbergers turned in their briefcases, left rush-hour commutes behind, and assumed the lives of vintners in the Paso Robles wine country.

Midnight Cellars had its beginnings in a "half-serious" comment made during a 1994 family wine-tasting trip to Northern California. Rich said to Bob, "Dad, why don't you buy a winery, and Michelle and I will help you run it." On the spot, Mike offered his services too. A year later, Rich, Michelle, and Mike were delighted and surprised when Bob and Mary Jane bought a 150-acre ranch in the hills of west Paso Robles. "The acreage offered everything we were looking for," Bob explains. "The Paso Robles area had a worldwide recognition for producing ultra-premium wines, and we found a close-knit, cooperative atmosphere among winery owners and winemakers."

The family transformed the property's barley field into a vineyard, planting their first vines in 1996. A large horse barn was converted into a winery, and during the fermentation process the Hartenbergers frequently "burned the midnight oil"— their toils into the wee hours inspired the winery's name.

Midnight Cellars hit the ground running, earning numerous medals for its first releases at wine competitions throughout the state and country. Recently, Midnight's Chardonnay took home a bronze medal at the 2004 New World International Wine Competition, its Full Moon Red won a gold at the 2004 Pacific Rim International Wine Competition, and its Estate Zinfandel received a gold at the 2004 West Coast Wine Competition.

In 2000, the Hartenbergers constructed a new, 10,000-square-foot, state-of-the-art winery that contains a laboratory, barrel room, and tank room to allow complete control of the winemaking process.

Midnight Cellars
2925 Anderson Road
Paso Robles, CA 93446
(805) 239-8904
info@midnightcellars.com
www.midnightcellars.com

Sub-AVA: Paso Robles

Owners: The Hartenberger family

Tasting Hours:
10 a.m. – 5:30 p.m. daily

Wines: Syrah, Zinfandel, Cabernet Sauvignon, Merlot, Chardonnay, Sangiovese, blends

Winemaker's Specialty: Zinfandel

Winemaker: Richard Hartenberger

Thai Beef Salad

2 green onions, chopped
1 c. lemon grass, cut into 1-inch pieces
1 c. each fresh cilantro and mint leaves, chopped
1 c. lime juice
1/3 c. fish sauce
1 Tbsp. sweet chili sauce
1/2 c. white sugar
1-1/2 lbs. 1-inch-thick steak fillet
1 head leaf lettuce, torn into bite-size pieces
1/2 English cucumber, diced
1 pt. cherry tomatoes

In a large bowl, stir together green onions, lemon grass, cilantro, mint leaves, lime juice, fish sauce, chili sauce, and sugar until well combined and sugar is dissolved. Set sauce mixture aside. Grill steak over high heat for approximately 4 to 6 minutes on each side, until medium done. Remove from grill and slice into thin strips. Add meat with its juices to sauce mixture, cover, and refrigerate at least 3 hours. Place lettuce in a salad bowl, arrange cucumber on top of lettuce, and pour the meat and sauce over all. Top with the cherry tomatoes and garnish with fresh cilantro leaves. Serve with **Midnight Cellars Estate Zinfandel**.

NORMAN VINEYARDS

Art Norman's passion for viticulture stems from his childhood memories of home winemaking with his father and grandfather. Many years later, Art's early love for making wine led him to found Norman Vineyards, which has been the focus of his life ever since.

"I was working as an engineer in the Southern California aerospace industry when my winemaking memories got the best of me," Art remembers. In 1971, he and his wife, Lei, purchased 40 acres on Vineyard Drive in the then-undiscovered west side of Paso Robles. The Normans planted Zinfandel, Merlot, Cabernet, Cabernet Franc, and Barbera vines. For the next 20 years, Norman Vineyards grew premium grapes that were purchased by local wineries.

More than 20 years after he planted his vineyards, and almost half a century since his winemaking days with his father and grandfather, Art began to make wine—at the insistence of his customers. Many local wineries were consistently winning awards for the wines they produced from Norman Vineyard grapes. Finally, local winery owners banned together and told Art it was time for him to start making his own wine. In 1992, Norman Vineyards bottled its first vintage and constructed a tasting room adjacent to the vineyard.

Today, Art is a recognized pillar of the San Luis Obispo County wine industry, and he and Lei continue to be proud of Norman Vineyards' reputation as a family-oriented winery.

In the tasting room, the fireplace is often lighted in winter, and in any season guests are never shy about sitting down to play the piano. As a hands-on owner, Art not only oversees the winery operations but often mans the tasting bar, chatting with customers about his wines and his travels to meet customers in Switzerland and Japan and in the more than 45 states across America where Norman Vineyard vintages are sold.

Norman Vineyards
7450 Vineyard Drive
Paso Robles, CA 93446
(805) 237-0138
info@normanvineyards.com
www.normanvineyards.com

Sub-AVA: Paso Robles

Owners: Art and Lei Norman

Tasting Hours:
11 a.m. – 5 p.m. daily

Wines: Zinfandel, Meritage, Cabernet Sauvignon, Syrah, Chardonnay

Winemaker's Specialty: Zinfandel

Winemaker: Joe Kidd

Chili Night

10 oz. bacon, sliced into thin pieces
4 lbs. lamb stewing pieces
3 Tbsp. salad oil
1 each red pepper and onion, diced
1/4 c. red wine vinegar
3/4 gal. beef stock
2 qt. tomato juice
1 Tbsp. each sage, oregano, ground cumin, coriander
8 cloves garlic
1 jalapeño, minced
3 c. white beans, soaked in water and drained
4 c. Norman Vineyards Syrah
Salt and pepper to taste

In a large pot, sauté bacon and lamb in oil. Remove lamb and set aside. Sauté onion and pepper in bacon for 3 minutes. Add remaining ingredients, except the lamb. In a skillet, brown lamb pieces over high heat and add to the chili. Adjust seasonings and simmer over low heat until beans are tender. Enjoy with **Norman Vineyards Syrah**.

OPOLO VINEYARDS

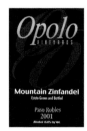

In the Santa Lucia Mountains just west of Paso Robles, a rustic road winds past a meandering creek and moss-draped oak trees and leads to the exquisitely tended grounds of Opolo Vineyards. High on the hillside behind the winery, vibrantly colored iceplant has been manicured to spell out "Opolo Vineyards" in an impressive natural display.

Opolo Vineyards comprises 300 acres of estate vineyards, 100 planted at the winery in the cool, maritime climate of the west hills of Adelaida, and 200 in the warmer temperatures of the east side of Paso Robles. These contrasting microclimates coupled with a variety of soils allow Opolo to grow a wide range of varietals, including Sangiovese, Zinfandel, Pinot Noir, Merlot, Cabernet Sauvignon, and Chardonnay.

Owners Rick Quinn and Dave Nichols believe great wine begins where the grapes are grown, and their focus is careful management of their vineyards. "Opolo's vineyards are well positioned to produce some of the finest ultra-premium wines from this stellar winegrowing region," Rick emphasizes. His partner, Dave, agrees: "These climatic variations allow a long 'hang time,' which yields high sugar levels, great fruit components, and excellent aging potential."

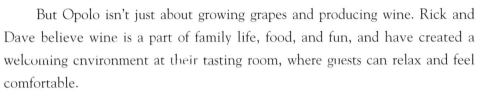

But Opolo isn't just about growing grapes and producing wine. Rick and Dave believe wine is a part of family life, food, and fun, and have created a welcoming environment at their tasting room, where guests can relax and feel comfortable.

On weekends, Opolo's friendly staff barbeques complimentary sausages for visitors, who are encouraged to enjoy the patio and take in the view. The winery also hosts quarterly barbeques, including a Serbian-style event that celebrates Rick's Serbian heritage and features roasted lamb, folk music, and dancing. A special highlight of the year is the annual "grape stomp," at which guests are invited to take off their shoes and help crush grapes the old-fashioned way.

Opolo Vineyards
7110 Vineyard Drive
Paso Robles, CA 93446
(805) 238-9593
sales@opolo.com
www.opolo.com

Sub-AVA: Paso Robles

Owners:
Rick Quinn, Dave Nichols

Tasting Hours:
11 a.m. – 5 p.m. daily

Wines: Zinfandel, Cabernet Sauvignon, Merlot, Sangiovese, Pinot Noir, Syrah, Viognier, Roussanne

Winemakers' Specialty:
Rhapsody Meritage blend

Winemakers:
Rick Quinn, Dave Nichols

Roast Pork Tenderloin with Dried-Cherry Syrah Reduction Sauce

1 lb. pork tenderloin, cut into 4 equal portions
1 c. Opolo Vineyards Syrah
1/4 c. dried cherries
1/8 c. brown sugar
1 c. veal or beef stock

Place dried cherries and syrah in a saucepan. Let soak for 1/2 hour. Place saucepan on medium heat and bring to simmer. Add brown sugar and stock and bring back to simmer. Simmer for 20 to 30 minutes, stirring occasionally until sauce slightly thickens and coats the back of a spoon. Grill tenderloin over open flame to desired doneness, approximately 4 minutes per side for medium. Top tenderloin with reduction sauce and serve with **Opolo Vineyards Syrah.**
Recipe courtesy Chef Chris Maritzen, Corner View Restaurant & Bar, San Luis Obispo

PEACHY CANYON WINERY

"Peachy Canyon Winery is all about quality, family, and friends," Doug Beckett insists. "It's a quality you can savor in every taste of our wine." Located among the rolling hills of Paso Robles, Peachy Canyon is owned and operated by Doug and his wife, Nancy, and their sons, Josh and Jake. Together, the Beckett family has created a winemaking legacy sure to be handed down through future generations of Beckett wine enthusiasts.

Family participation is a way of life at Peachy Canyon Winery. Jake, the vineyard manager, labors with his crew year round to produce the highest quality fruit. Most of the grapes that become Peachy Canyon wines come from the winery's five estate vineyards—Peachy Canyon Estate, Mustang Springs, Old School House, Snow, and Mustard Creek—which together comprise nearly 100 acres. The Becketts also source fruit from trusted grower-partners with whom they've had longstanding contracts.

Josh, the second-generation Beckett winemaker, focuses on bringing maximum flavor and balance to Peachy Canyon wines, while striving to make the highest quality wine at the most reasonable price on the Central Coast. Josh's skills have paid off richly: Peachy Canyon wines have received many awards, including recognition as a Top 10 wine value by the 2003 Chicago Value Wine Challenge. Beckett family wines were named the "Most Favorite Zinfandel" in the 2002 and 2003 Tribune Voters Choice Competition and earlier gained *Wine Spectator* magazine's recommendation as one of the top Zinfandels in 1990 and 1991.

Doug and Nancy, who founded Peachy Canyon Winery in 1982, travel the world sharing their internationally sold vintages with members of the wine trade and promoting the growing reputation of Central Coast vineyards and wineries. The Becketts firmly believe that the Central Coast—and the Paso Robles sub-AVA in particular—is one of the world's premier wine-grape regions.

The Peachy Canyon tasting room and gift shop makes its home in the circa-1886 Bethel Schoolhouse on scenic Highway 46 West, in a setting of rolling vineyards and native oak trees. The tasting room's park-like grounds include an old-fashioned gazebo where visitors can picnic and enjoy Peachy Canyon selections. "Gather 'round your family and friends," the Becketts are fond of saying. "We'll provide the wine."

Peachy Canyon Winery
1480 N. Bethel Road
Templeton, CA 93465
(805) 239-1918
peachy@tcsn.net
www.peachycanyonwinery.com

Sub-AVA: Paso Robles

Owners: Doug, Nancy, Josh, and Jake Beckett

Tasting Hours:
11 a.m. – 5 p.m. daily

Wines: Zinfandel, Cabernet Sauvignon, Merlot, Chardonnay, Sangiovese, Zinfandel Port

Winemaker's Specialty: Zinfandel

Winemaker: Josh Beckett

Taco Soup

1 onion, chopped
2 garlic cloves, chopped
1 Tbsp. cooking oil
1 lb. ground round (or soy substitute)
1 12-oz. bottle beer
1 can pinto beans, rinsed
1 can kidney beans, rinsed
2 c. chicken or vegetable broth
2 ripe tomatoes

1 14-1/2-oz. can corn, rinsed
Sour cream
Fresh chives, chopped

Sauté onion and garlic in oil. Add ground round and cook thoroughly. Add beer, beans, broth, tomatoes, and corn, and bring to a light boil. Pour into bowls and top with a dollop of sour cream and a sprinkling of chives. Serve with **Peachy Canyon Zinfandel.**

PIPESTONE VINEYARDS

Pipestone Vineyards operates in accordance with the principles of *feng shui*, the ancient Chinese philosophy that interprets how Earth energies co-exist and interact at specific locations. The small, family-owned winery, established in 1997 in a serene valley just west of Paso Robles, is owned by Jeff Pipes and Florence Wong, a husband-and-wife team who believe that harnessing this Earth energy can enhance everything from health to luck to the quality of the wine produced at their winery. Pipestone Vineyards may be the only winery and vineyard in California that is laid out and managed according to traditional *feng shui* precepts.

"We never would have purchased the property if it hadn't had a south-facing slope and hills to the north," says Jeff. "We planted the vineyard and built everything at the winery according to *feng shui*." The couple also farms by the Chinese calendar and practices organic farming techniques. Jeff and Florence believe organically cultivated soil produces healthier plants, creating a habitat for beneficial insects that protect the vineyard and eliminate the need for insecticides or herbicides.

"Pipestone Vineyards produces southern Rhône-style wines because we love the way these varietals pair with the Mediterranean and Asian food we eat," explains Florence. "Food and family are an important part of our lives, so producing wines that complement our own cooking seemed like the obvious thing to do." Approximately 80 percent of Pipestone's production is red wine varietals—Syrah, Grenache, Zinfandel, and Rhône-style blends—while the remainder is Viognier.

In addition to growing grapes and making wine, Jeff and Florence operate a small farm on their 30-acre property. Farm animals—Lucy the goat, chickens, ducks, geese, and pigeons—share the land with beehives and almond, walnut, and olive trees. A lavender garden provides the natural filler for Jeff and Florence's two young daughters to create lavender sachets, which are sold at the Pipestone gift shop. Also featured are farm-fresh eggs, honey, olives, olive oil, nuts, and Florence's prize-winning homemade Syrah and Chardonnay jellies.

Pipestone Vineyards
2040 Niderer Rd.
Paso Robles, CA 93446
(805) 227-6385
www.pipestonevineyards.com

Sub-AVA: Paso Robles

Owners:
Jeff Pipes and Florence Wong

Tasting Hours:
11 a.m. – 5 p.m. Thursday – Monday

Wines: Viognier, Syrah, Grenache, Zinfandel, Rhône-style blends

Winemaker's Specialty:
Rhône-style blends

Winemaker: Jeff Pipes

Penne with Peppers and Sausage

4 mild Italian sausages, casings removed and meat crumbled
1 large clove garlic, peeled and cut in half
3 Tbsp. olive oil
1/2 medium yellow onion, chopped
1 each large red and yellow bell peppers, cubed
1 20-oz. can Italian peeled tomatoes with juice, coarsely chopped
1/2 tsp. each salt and freshly ground pepper
Pinch red pepper flakes
2 Tbsp. unsalted butter, melted
2/3 c. Parmesan cheese, freshly grated
1 lb. ridged penne pasta, cooked *al dente*

In a large saucepan over medium heat, sauté garlic in olive oil until browned. Discard garlic. Add onions and peppers and cook about 7 minutes or until onion is wilted. Add tomatoes with their juice, 1 c. water, salt, pepper, and red pepper flakes, and cook about 10 minutes. Place sausage and 1/4 c. water in a skillet and cook over medium heat until sausage is browned and water has evaporated. Add sausage along with 3 Tbsp. of pan drippings to sauce mixture. Cook over medium heat for 10 minutes. Add butter and cheese to pasta and toss with sauce. Serve with **Pipestone Vineyards Grenache**.
Recipe courtesy Chef Debbie Duggan, Central Coast Culinary and Catering, San Luis Obispo

PRETTY SMITH VINEYARDS & WINERY

People often think of Lisa Pretty as a Renaissance woman who almost single-handedly operates Pretty Smith Vineyards & Winery in San Miguel. As the owner of the winery and one of the few female winemakers in San Luis Obispo County, Lisa manages sales, marketing, accounting, and the tasting bar, as well as the cultivation of her 45-acre vineyard that was planted with Bordeaux varietals in 1980. Lisa mows and sprays the fields herself and only hires help to prune the vines and harvest the grapes.

Lisa became interested in winemaking as a child growing up in Canada. She recalls, "Wine was served with special meals and the children were allowed to taste it as a treat." As an adult, Lisa began to make wine using homemade winemaking kits. Today, she produces her signature "Palette de Rouge" and other Bordeaux-style blends because she believes "it's the style people really like" and that "winemakers express their creativity by blending together different varietals."

Lisa also shows her creative side in packaging her wines. Every year, Pretty Smith wines display a new series

of labels, made from Lisa's original oil paintings of American Indian images. She is particularly fond of the mythical figure Kokopelli, who dances along the hilltops and rocky buttes of the Southwest playing his flute to entice the sun to rise each day. Kokopelli is known for promoting abundance and fertility, which is a predominant theme of Pretty Smith's Southwestern-style tasting room.

Among Pretty Smith's many accolades are a silver medal at the 2004 Riverside International Wine Competition for its 2000 Cabernet Sauvignon, a silver medal at the 2003 San Diego National Wine Competition for its 2001 Palette de Blanc, and a rating of 87 points from the Beverage Testing Institute for its 1999 Zinfandel Port, 2000 Cabernet Franc, and 2000 Merlot.

Pretty Smith Vineyards & Winery
13350 North River Road
San Miguel, CA 93451
(805) 467-3104
info@prettysmith.com
www.prettysmith.com

Sub-AVA: Paso Robles

Owners:
Lisa Pretty, Victor Smith

Tasting Hours:
10 a.m. – 5 p.m. Friday – Sunday

Wines: Palette de Rouge blend, Merlot, Cabernet Franc, Cabernet Sauvignon, Sauvignon Blanc

Winemaker's Specialty:
Palette de Rouge blend

Winemaker: Lisa Pretty

Pretty Grilled Vegetables

4 heads baby bok choy
1 each green and red bell peppers, seeded and cut into 4 large pieces
1 large sweet onion, cut in half to form large rings
1 bundle asparagus
1 package small portabello mushrooms, cleaned and de-stemmed
1/2 c. olive oil
1/4 c. soy sauce
1/4 c. Pretty-Smith Cabernet Franc
2 Tbsp. fresh basil, chopped, or 1 Tbsp. dried

1 Tbsp. each fresh thyme and oregano, chopped, or 1-1/2 tsp. dried
3 cloves garlic, crushed
1 Tbsp. celery seed

Place vegetables in a large bowl and set aside. Mix together the remaining ingredients, pour over vegetables, and stir. Marinate mixture for 2 to 6 hours, stirring every hour or two. Grill over medium flame in a vegetable basket or barbeque meshed plate for 8 minutes, stirring often. Serve over noodles or rice and with **Pretty Smith Cabernet Franc**.

(Photo at left by Michael Urbanek)

RABBIT RIDGE WINERY & VINEYARDS

When Erich Russell competed as a world-class track star at California State University, San Jose, he often set the pace, taking the lead quickly and holding it to the finish line. Dubbed "The Rabbit" by his teammates, Erich never imagined his running style would someday mirror his rapid success in the winery business.

After graduation, Erich taught high school track and field in San Diego, and in his off hours at home pursued his interest in winemaking. When a Sonoma County vintner praised Erich's homemade wine at a 1979 amateur winemaking contest, Erich quit his teaching job and went to work at Chateau St. Jean Winery in Kenwood, Calif.

In 1981, Erich founded Rabbit Ridge Winery in Healdsburg, Calif. "Rabbit Ridge gained a reputation as one of the area's top wineries in both volume and quality," Erich says. By the mid-1990s, Rabbit Ridge had outgrown its facility. Realizing Sonoma County's escalating land prices were reflected in the elevated prices of many of the area's wine grapes, Erich purchased property in west Paso Robles. "In my new location," Erich explains, "I could grow high-quality grapes and produce better wines at reasonable prices." In 1997, Erich planted the first of Rabbit Ridge's four vineyards.

Construction of a new, 55,000-square-foot, three-story winery was completed in 2003. The building's high-tech design uses gravity and the property's sloping hillside to transfer the fresh grape juice to different areas within the winery. Grapes are crushed at the top of the hill on the crush pad and gravity brings the juice down to the tank room 22 feet below. After fermentation, the wine is gravity fed another 22 feet to the barrel room.

"The use of gravity flow is gentler on the grapes and helps preserve the quality of our wines," says Erich. A computer operates and monitors all tanks so the temperature and fermentation rate are precisely controlled. "This process gives us full control of all aspects of winemaking and ensures consistent quality," Erich says.

Rabbit Ridge Winery & Vineyards
1172 San Marcos Road
Paso Robles, CA 93446
(805) 467-3331
rabbitridgewines@yahoo.com
www.rabbitridgewinery.com

Sub-AVA: Paso Robles

Owners: Erich and Joanne Russell

Tasting Hours:
Noon – 5 p.m. daily

Wines: Zinfandel, Syrah, Viognier, Pinot Noir, Chardonnay, Primitivo blend

Winemaker's Specialties:
Zinfandel, Primitivo, Vortex blends

Winemaker: Erich Russell

Crabmeat on Belgian Endive

2 Tbsp. butter
4 cloves garlic, minced
2 shallots, minced
8 oz. cream cheese, softened
3 oz. goat cheese, softened
1 tsp. garlic powder
1/2 tsp. Lawry's seasoning salt
1 tsp. each fresh, parsley, dill, and basil, minced
1/2 tsp. fresh thyme, minced
1 c. fresh lump crabmeat
2 Tbsp. mayonnaise
5 heads Belgian endive, separated into leaves
1 large red pepper, diced
Alfalfa sprouts for garnish

Sauté garlic and shallots in butter. Place in a food processor with cheeses and seasonings. Mix thoroughly. Place mixture in a bowl and add herbs, stirring to combine. Combine mayonnaise and cheese mixture. Gently fold in crabmeat. Spread crab mixture on endive leaves, top with pepper and sprouts. Chill 30 minutes. Serve with **Rabbit Ridge Sauvignon Blanc** or **Chardonnay**.

RIO SECO VINEYARD & WINERY

Rio Seco Vineyard & Winery owners Tom and Carol Hinkle are proud that they're "a comfortable mom-and-pop winery with fine wines and friendly people." Longtime San Luis Obispo County residents, the Hinkles entered the world of viticulture as "an ultimate retirement dream" after completing successful teaching careers, Tom at California Polytechnic State University in San Luis Obispo and Carol at two local high schools.

In 1996, Tom and Carol purchased 64 acres near the dry bed of Huerjuero Creek in east Paso Robles. They named their winery "Rio Seco"—"Dry River" in Spanish. The following spring, Tom and Carol planted a 30-acre vineyard that today produces the fruit for their award-winning estate wines. "Our fruit is intensely flavorful because we semi- dry farm our vineyard," says Carol.

The Hinkles don't add chemicals to their wines nor do they use stainless steel tanks. All wines are barrel fermented and red varietals are allowed to age for almost two years before bottling. "We have so much good fruit to work with, we only use neutral oak barrels so as not to mask the flavors," explains Carol.

Rio Seco has achieved critical acclaim for its Rhône-style varietals. In 2004, its 2001 Syrah received a gold medal at the Orange County Fair Wine Competition. Its 2002 Roussanne won a bronze medal at the Monterey Wine Competition and a silver at the Riverside International Wine Competition.

Although the Hinkles are "retired," that doesn't stop Tom from pursuing his other passion—baseball. When Tom isn't managing the vineyard, making award-winning wine, or manning the tasting bar, he works as a scout for professional baseball teams. Tom always has interesting baseball stories to share with his guests at the tasting room, and he's especially proud of Rio Seco's "Diamond Club." The wine club benefits the Professional Baseball Scouts Foundation, which provides monetary assistance to baseball scouts and their families in the event of catastrophic illness or a medical emergency.

Each week all summer, except during the run of the Mid-State Fair, Rio Seco hosts a "Friday Fun Night." Guests are invited to bring meats and vegetables for the grill or purchase a barbequed meal prepared by Tom. Complimentary wine tasting and live music are also part of the fun.

Rio Seco Vineyard & Winery
4295 Union Road
Paso Robles, CA 93446
(805) 237-8884
rioseco@tcsn.net
www.riosecowine.com

Sub-AVA: Paso Robles

Owners: Tom and Carol Hinkle

Tasting Hours:
11 a.m. – 5:30 p.m. Thursday – Monday

Wines: Cabernet Sauvignon, Cabernet Franc, Syrah, Zinfandel, Roussanne, Viognier

Winemaker's Specialties: Cabernet Sauvignon, Cabernet Franc

Winemaker: Tom Hinkle

Smoked Black Olives

1 c. black olives, Greek or Spanish, lightly drained
1 c. green olives, lightly drained
2 Tbsp. extra virgin olive oil
2 Tbsp. Rio Seco white wine (Roussanne works well)
2 cloves garlic, minced
3/4 tsp. dried oregano
Rosemary sprigs to taste
Salt and freshly ground black pepper to taste

Prepare a smoker for barbequing, bringing the temperature to 200° to 220°. Arrange the olives in a shallow, smoke-proof dish or in a piece of heavy-duty foil molded into a small tray. Add the remaining ingredients. Place the olives in the smoker and cook until the olives absorb half the liquid and take on a light smoke flavor, approximately 55 to 60 minutes. Olives can be served immediately or can sit for several hours to develop further flavors. Leftovers may be refrigerated. Enjoy with **Rio Seco Syrah**.

ROBERT HALL WINERY

When native Minnesotan Robert Hall completed his successful military career, he turned to business, acquiring shopping centers, bowling alleys, champion horses, and travel agencies. His involvement with the travel industry led him to explore his increasing interest in wine and the world's many grape-growing regions. During a late-1970s trip to the south of France, Robert became so impressed with the Rhône varietals that he decided to start his own winery and began to study wine-producing areas in the United States.

On a visit to Paso Robles, he found soils, climate, and geography similar to those of the Rhône Valley. In the early 1990s, Robert purchased property in east Paso Robles, and in 1995—on the rolling hills north of the Estrella Plain—planted Home Vineyard, the first of Robert Hall Winery's three estate vineyards. Robert then purchased two pieces of adjacent land that became the Bench and Terrace vineyards.

In 2002, Robert opened the enormous Robert Hall Winery "to use time-tested techniques and practices to cultivate intensely colored and flavored grapes and to produce rich, mid-priced, Rhône-style estate wines that capture the essence of Paso Robles."

Robert attributes the success of Robert Hall Winery to his passion for wine and his years of business experience, and to Don Brady, his winemaker, and the rest of the Robert Hall team. "You build a business on team effort," explains Robert, "and we have a marvelous team."

Robert Hall's 12,000-square-foot Mediterranean-style tasting room is complemented by cascading fountains, a 90-foot-long mirror pond, and a 45-foot-high tower enclosing an elevator that descends to wine caves 10 feet below ground level. Nearly 19,000 square feet of rambling caves provide storage space and a constant temperature of 55 to 60 degrees.

"In the caves the wine has a chance to relax, mature, and come together," Robert says. "That's one of our successes in winemaking." The cave walls—faux-finished to resemble granite—and custom-made light fixtures create an elegant setting for winemaker dinners, weddings, and special events.

Behind the tasting room, a 200-seat amphitheater provides a spacious venue for concerts and plays.

Robert Hall Winery
3443 Mill Road
Paso Robles, CA 93446
(805) 239-1616
info@roberthallwinery.com
www.roberthallwinery.com

Sub-AVA: Paso Robles

Owners:
Robert Hall, Margaret Burrell

Tasting Hours:
10 a.m. – 6 p.m. daily (Summer)
10 a.m. – 5 p.m. daily (Winter)

Wines: Rhone de Robles, Syrah, Cabernet Sauvignon, Zinfandel, Merlot, Rosé de Robles, Sauvignon Blanc, Meritage, Chardonnay, port

Winemaker's Specialty:
Rhone de Robles

Winemaker: Don Brady

Feta-Basil Shrimp in Wine

2 lbs. large shrimp, shelled and deveined
2 Tbsp. olive oil
2 tsp. garlic, minced
1/4 to 1/2 c. dry white wine
1 14-oz. can crushed tomatoes with juice, coarsely chopped
1 tsp. each, salt and freshly ground pepper
8 oz. feta cheese, crumbled
3 Tbsp. fresh basil, chopped

Heat olive oil in a heavy saucepan over medium heat and sauté garlic until fragrant, 1 to 2 minutes. Add wine, simmer for 2 minutes. Add tomatoes and simmer 15 minutes. Place shrimp in a baking dish, sprinkle with salt and pepper. Top with feta cheese. Sprinkle half the basil over the cheese. Pour tomato sauce over all, cover with foil, and bake for 15 minutes at 350°. Remove dish from oven and sprinkle with remaining basil. Serve over rice. Enjoy with **Robert Hall Rhone de Robles**.

SAN MARCOS CREEK VINEYARD

Fling and Annette Traylor were high school sweethearts who nearly 50 years later developed a love of wine. In the early 1990s, the Traylors' retirement plans took them to Paso Robles, where they could "take advantage of the area's increasing reputation for growing premium wine grapes and also have some fun and excitement." The Traylors purchased land just north of town and planted a 40-acre vineyard. In 1992, they established San Marcos Creek Vineyard and soon negotiated contracts to sell grapes to several local, premium wineries.

By 2002, Fling and Annette's "retirement" included winemaking, the construction of a winery and tasting room, and future plans for a bed and breakfast. Their daughter and son-in-law, Catherine and Brady Winter, joined them as partners in the family business—Catherine as the bookkeeper and tasting room manager, and Brady as the winery manager and one of two resident winemakers.

San Marcos Creek's state-of-the-art winery includes a fully equipped laboratory and barrel room, and specializes in small quantities of single-vineyard estate Bordeaux, Italian, and Rhône- and California-style wines. Most varietals are aged for up to three years in French and American oak barrels. "This aging process allows the wines to develop the proper flavor and structure," Fling explains.

San Marcos Creek's French country-style tasting room opened in 2004. The only tasting room in San Luis Obispo County located right on Highway 101, the handsome facility is constructed of stone and provides scenic views of the estate vineyards. Guests can sample San Marcos Creek's current releases at the elegant, wood-paneled tasting bar, browse the gift shop, or relax under an umbrella with a glass of wine at one of the terrace's picnic tables. A private tasting room is available for small groups, and winemaker dinners are offered in the intimacy of the 1,000-square-foot wine cellar.

San Marcos Creek Vineyard
7750 North Highway 101
Paso Robles, CA 93446
(805) 467-2670
brady@sanmarcoscreek.com
www.sanmarcoscreek.com

Sub-AVA: Paso Robles

Owners:
Fling and Annette Traylor,
Brady and Catherine Winter

Tasting Hours:
11 a.m. – 6 p.m. daily

Wines: Viognier, White Merlot, Nebbiolo, Merlot, Zinfandel, Late Harvest Zinfandel, Syrah, Cabernet Sauvignon

Winemakers' Specialties:
Syrah, Nebbiolo

Winemakers:
Brady Winter, Paul Ayres

Individual Molten Chocolate Cakes

7-1/2 oz. bittersweet chocolate, coarsely chopped
11 Tbsp. unsalted butter, cut into large pieces
3 large eggs
3 large egg yolks
1/4 c. plus 2 Tbsp. granulated sugar
5 Tbsp. sifted flour
Powdered sugar, for garnish
1 pt. fresh raspberries

Butter and lightly flour six 6-oz. custard cups. Place 5-1/2 oz. chocolate and the butter in a metal bowl that has been set over a pan of simmering hot water; stir until melted and smooth. Cool slightly. Beat eggs, the yolks, and granulated sugar with an electric mixer at medium-high speed until thick and pale, about 10 minutes. Reduce speed; gradually mix in flour. Add chocolate mixture to flour and beat until thick and glossy, about 5 minutes. Pour half the mixture into the custard cups, add 1 Tbsp. remaining chocolate chunks to each cup, and top with remaining mixture. Bake at 325° for about 12 minutes, until edges are set but center jiggles slightly. Cool 5 minutes, run knife around outside edge of cup, and invert on individual plates. Sprinkle with sifted powdered sugar and raspberries. Enjoy with **San Marcos Creek Late Harvest Zinfandel.**

SUMMERWOOD WINERY

One of the striking sights along Highway 46 West in Paso Robles is Summerwood Winery. Adjacent to the impressive New England-style Summerwood Inn, the picturesque winery stands among well-manicured estate vineyards, white picket fences, and colorful gardens that span the frontage of the 46-acre property.

Summerwood's elegant tasting room boasts a polished marble bar, slate and African mahogany floors, overstuffed chairs, a fireplace, and French doors that open to an expansive brick patio and a garden gazebo.

The winery's densely planted estate vineyards receive minimal irrigation and yield a low-volume crop, which winemaker Scott Hawley believes "maximizes varietal character and intensity." A moisture sensor that downloads data onto his laptop computer allows Scott to determine optimal irrigation times. Cover crops and compost and the creation of beneficial insect habitats eliminate insecticide use and enhance the health and longevity of the soil and vineyard.

Harvest times are determined by the flavor and physiological maturity of the grapes rather than by their sugar concentration. Fruit is hand sorted and gravity fed into custom-made fermentation tanks and basket presses, eliminating the need for mechanical pumping. All Summerwood wines age in oak barrels and are sold only at the tasting room.

At the 2004 Critics Challenge International Wine Competition, Summerwood received top honors for its Sentio III 2001, the Critics Gold for its 2001 Diosa, and the Critics Award for its 2002 Diosa.

Just a few steps from the winery, the Summerwood Inn offers guests luxurious comfort. Nine spacious and tastefully decorated guest rooms feature gas fireplaces and private balconies with vineyard views. Amenities include plush terrycloth robes and nightly bed turn-down service. Visitors enjoy cooked-to-order breakfasts, daily homemade desserts, and each afternoon complimentary Summerwood wine served with gourmet appetizers.

Summerwood Winery
2175 Arbor Road
Paso Robles, CA 93446
(805) 227-1365
info@summerwoodwine.com
www.summerwoodwine.com

Sub-AVA: Paso Robles

Owner:
Summerwood Winery & Inn, Inc.

Tasting Hours:
10 a.m. – 6 p.m. daily (Summer)
10 a.m. – 5:30 p.m. daily (Winter)

Wines: Bordeaux- and Rhône-style blends, Cabernet Sauvignon, Syrah, Vin Rouge, Zinfandel, Viognier, Chardonnay, port

Winemaker's Specialties:
Sentio Bordeaux-style blend, Diosa Rhône-style blend

Winemaker: Scott Hawley

Osso Bucco

6 lamb shanks, cut 1 inch thick
1 c. all-purpose flour
1 Tbsp. sea salt
1 tsp. freshly ground white pepper
1/4 c. extra virgin olive oil
2 c. each celery, onion, carrot, diced into
    1/4-inch pieces
2 Tbsp. minced garlic
1 bottle Summerwood red wine
1 12-oz. can Italian plum tomatoes
6 sprigs fresh rosemary
12 sprigs fresh thyme

Mix flour, salt, and pepper. Lightly coat lamb in flour mixture. In a skillet, brown lamb in olive oil over medium heat. Place lamb in a braising pan or casserole dish. Add vegetables and garlic to skillet and sauté, scraping up brown bits. Add wine to skillet and bring to a boil. Add cut-up tomatoes and juice to skillet and stir. Pour the vegetable mixture over the lamb and top with rosemary and thyme sprigs. Cover and bake at 350° for 2-1/2 hours until meat falls off the bones. Place meat on a serving dish. Reduce vegetable sauce over high heat, constantly stirring, until thick. Pour sauce over the meat and serve with **Summerwood Sentio**.
Recipe courtesy Charles Paladin Wayne, executive chef, Summerwood Winery & Inn

SYLVESTER VINEYARDS & WINERY

In the early 1960s, Austrian-born businessman Sylvester Feichtinger purchased Rancho Robles, a 430-acre cattle ranch and hay farm just north of Paso Robles. In his free time, Sylvester enjoyed making fruit wines, a love that set the stage for his longtime dream of one day opening a winery. In 1982, he planted a vineyard on part of the ranch property, and in the following years sold grapes to local premium wineries.

In 1990, Sylvester released his first wines under the Sylvester Vineyards & Winery label and began plans for a high-tech winery and tasting room, a project that was completed in time for the 1995 harvest. The winery, which can make 50,000 cases a year, was designed to take advantage of the newest technologies and at the same time offer artisan wines that feature the Paso Robles *terroir*.

Sylvester Vineyards & Winery produces varietals from the Tuscan regions of Italy and the Bordeaux and Rhône regions of France. The winery also bottles reserve lots of dessert wines and ports, which are created in small quantities and sold almost exclusively at the tasting room. "Time-honored tradition, state-of-the-art technology, plant and soil harmony, and true passion for wine are the four things that make my wines so special," explains Sylvester. "We craft our wines to be approachable, with a bouquet that highlights the fruit, and a nose that's tempered with oak aromas."

The bright and spacious tasting room features gift items, crystal, wine accessories, logoed apparel, and a large assortment of gourmet meats and cheeses that are perfect for an impromptu picnic on the tasting-room patio. Behind the tasting room, guests can visit the bygone era of luxurious rail travel at the train-car museum, which includes two vintage Pullman sleepers and a dining car.

Sylvester Vineyards & Winery
5115 Buena Vista Drive
Paso Robles, CA 93446
(805) 227-4000
(800) 891-6055 toll free
info@sylvesterwinery.com
www.sylvesterwinery.com

Sub-AVA: Paso Robles

Owner: Sylvester Feichtinger

Tasting Hours:
11 a.m. – 5 p.m. Monday – Thursday
10 a.m. – 5 p.m. Friday – Sunday

Wines: Zinfandel, Cabernet Sauvignon, Merlot, Syrah, Sangiovese, Chardonnay

Winemakers' Specialty: Zinfandel

Winemakers:
Jac Jacobs, Michael Barreto

Roasted Tomato Bolognese with Wild Boar Sausage

5 lbs. fresh tomatoes, cut in half
1 large onion, peeled and cut into quarters
1 head of garlic, peeled (each clove bruised lightly with flat part of a knife)
3 fresh poblano chilies with seeds, cut in quarters
1 large summer squash, chopped
1 sprig fresh rosemary
1/4 c. olive oil
1/4 c. balsamic vinegar
1 lb. wild boar sausage or Italian sausage, cooked and cut into bite-size pieces
1 c. fresh basil leaves, chopped (save a sprig for garnish)
1/2 c. fresh Italian parsley, minced (save a sprig for garnish)

Salt and pepper to taste
1 lb. cooked linguine
Freshly grated Parmesan cheese

Place tomatoes, onion, garlic, chilies, squash, and rosemary in a large baking pan. Drizzle with oil and vinegar and sprinkle with pepper. Bake uncovered at 350° for 1 to 2 hours until onions and garlic are soft and golden. Remove rosemary sprig and purée small batches of the sauce in a blender. Transfer sauce to a bowl; add cooked sausage, basil, and parsley. Taste and adjust seasonings, adding salt if necessary. Serve over hot linguine and top with cheese, basil, and parsley sprigs. Serve with **Sylvester Cabernet Sauvignon.**

TABLAS CREEK VINEYARD

The Châteauneuf-du-Pape appellation in France's southern Rhône Valley is world famous for its prized grapes and award-wining wines. Paso Robles offers its own flavor of the renowned French region at Tablas Creek Vineyard, where Rhône-style varietals and Châteauneuf-du-Pape-style blends are produced from grapevines imported directly from their native French growing ground, whose name means "New Palace of the Pope."

In the late 1980s, three friends formed a partnership to establish a winery in California where they could produce Châteauneuf-du-Pape varietals. Brothers Jean-Pierre and François Perrin, of the esteemed Château de Beaucastel winery in Châteauneuf-du-Pape, and well-known American wine-importer Robert Haas of Vineyard Brands searched extensively for vineyard land with soil and climate like the southern Rhône Valley's. In 1989, they established Tablas Creek Vineyard on 120 acres in the west hills of Paso Robles, 13 miles from the Pacific Ocean. The steep hillsides, rocky limestone soil, and Mediterranean climate reminded the three partners of the grape-growing conditions at Château de Beaucastel.

Jean-Pierre, François, and Robert then began importing grapevines from Châteauneuf-du-Pape. For three years, all the vines were held in quarantine, as required by the U.S. Bureau of Alcohol, Tobacco, and Firearms. In 1994, the partners planted their first vineyard, using the 100 percent organic farming techniques they still employ today. Tablas Creek Vineyard's first vintage was released in 1997, the same year the winery was constructed.

To propagate the French vine stock in sufficient numbers to plant its vineyard, Tablas Creek built its own grapevine nursery complex, the only on-site winery nursery in California. In the state-of-the-art green and shade houses, clones are grafted onto phylloxera-resistant rootstock. The vines are then planted at Tablas Creek Vineyard or sold to the public or to more than 100 vineyard customers across the United States.

The winery staff at Tablas Creek enjoys educating visitors through demonstrations, nursery and vineyard tours, winemaker dinners, and special events. Special hands-on seminars in organic farming teach guests to create and cultivate their own organic gardens, mix compost, and use predatory insects for crop protection, while how-to wine seminars provide lessons in do-it-yourself wine blending.

Tablas Creek Vineyard
9339 Adelaida Road
Paso Robles, CA 93446
(805) 237-1231
info@tablascreek.com
www.tablascreek.com

Sub-AVA: Paso Robles

Owners: Robert Haas,
Jean-Pierre Perrin, François Perrin

Tasting Hours:
10 a.m. – 5 p.m. daily

Wines: Esprit de Beaucastel, Esprit de Beaucastel Blanc, Côtes de Tablas, Côtes de Tablas Blanc, Roussanne

Winemaker's Specialties:
Esprit de Beaucastel, Esprit de Beaucastel Blanc, Panoplie

Winemaker: Neil Collins

Grilled Sea Scallops with Apples

12 large sea scallops
2 Granny Smith apples, cored and peeled
4 Tbsp. olive oil
1/4 c. seasoned rice vinegar
1/4 c. honey
8 fresh basil leaves, thinly sliced
Salt and freshly ground pepper

Preheat a gas grill at high heat. Slice apples crosswise into 1/4-inch slices. Brush olive oil on both sides of apple slices and scallops, and season lightly with salt and pepper. Grill apple slices for 1 minute on each side. Remove from heat and place 3 apple slices on each dinner plate. Grill scallops for 2 minutes on each side, and place a scallop on each grilled apple slice. Mix the rice vinegar and honey together and drizzle on scallops. Sprinkle with sliced basil and serve with freshly ground pepper and **Tablas Creek Esprit de Beaucastel Blanc**.
Recipe courtesy Chef Maegen Loring, The Park Restaurant, San Luis Obispo

TOBIN JAMES CELLARS

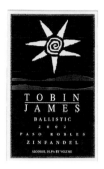

The notorious James Gang is alive and well and doing business at Tobin James Cellars in Paso Robles. The western-themed winery, renowned for its fun-loving attitude, high-spirited winery events, and down-to-earth, friendly staff, is a definite "must-see" for wine tasters. But don't be fooled—Tobin James is as serious about making wine as it is about having fun.

Built on the site of an 1860s Wells Fargo stagecoach stop, Tobin James Cellars was founded in 1987 by Tobin "Toby" James, who describes himself as "a true country boy." Toby had two prime objectives when he entered the wine business: to make excellent wine and to create an unpretentious winery that reflected his Midwestern roots, a place where people could relax and have fun. He constructed the Tobin James Cellars tasting room around a large, solid-mahogany, antique bar from a circa-1860s Missouri saloon that was regularly frequented by outlaw Jesse James.

In 1996, Lance and Claire Silver became co-owners of Tobin James Cellars. In the years that followed, the new partnership combined Toby's winemaking talents and the Silvers' business experience to enhance the winery's growing reputation and vastly widen its loyal clientele, providing old and new Tobin James customers with consistently good wines at great values.

The James Gang Wine Club is one of the largest in the world, with more than 10,000 members across the United States. "The winery doesn't advertise," Lance explains. "Our customers have built our reputation by word of mouth."

Wine club members are invited to stay overnight at the beautifully restored "stagecoach cottage," which functions as Tobin James' multi-roomed guesthouse and offers wine aficionados a truly memorable lodging experience. The gang at Tobin James claim they're not a B & B—a bed and breakfast—but a B & D—a "bed and directions" to breakfast. Whimsically painted bright yellow, the facility boasts a wraparound porch and three guest suites—each decorated in a different country-style theme—with plush feather beds and Egyptian cotton sheets, refrigerators, and private baths, two of which have Jacuzzi tubs.

Tobin James Cellars
8950 Union Road
Paso Robles, CA 93446
(805) 239-2204
info@tobinjames.com
www.tobinjames.com

Sub-AVA: Paso Robles

Owners:
Tobin James, Lance and Claire Silver

Tasting Hours:
10 a.m. – 6 p.m. daily

Wines: Zinfandel, Syrah, Cabernet Sauvignon, Chardonnay, Merlot, dessert wines

Winemakers' Specialty: Zinfandel

Winemakers:
Tobin James, Lance Silver, Jeff Poe

Gorgonzola-Pecan Ravioli with Sage Butter

1 pkg. egg roll skins
8 oz. crumbled Gorgonzola cheese
Chopped pecans, to taste
4 oz. salted butter, melted
Fresh sage, chopped

Heat a pot of water to just boiling. Mix butter and sage and set aside. Combine cheese and pecans. Cover a flat surface with wax paper and lay out egg roll skins. Top each skin with 1 Tbsp. cheese mixture and fold into triangle shapes. Using your fingertips, wet edges with warm water and press to seal. Gently submerge raviolis, one at a time, into just-boiling water for 30 to 60 seconds. Remove with a slotted spoon and brush with sage butter. Serve with **Tobin James Ballistic Zinfandel**.

VILLICANA WINERY

Some of life's most rewarding events happen serendipitously, the result of an altered plan, a change of course, or an unexpected set of circumstances. After college graduation, Alex Villicana enrolled in culinary school, intent on pursuing his interest in food and wine. But before Alex could begin his training as a gourmet chef, the school closed down, setting in motion a series of fateful happenings that ultimately led Alex to the 1993 founding of Villicana Winery in the west hills of Paso Robles.

After the culinary school's demise, Alex redirected his attention toward winemaking. He accepted a job harvesting grapes at a Paso Robles winery while he took several viticulture and enology classes through the University of California, Davis. Two years later, Alex "caught the winemaking bug" when he made his first vintage from grapes given to him by several local vineyards.

Soon, Alex began to lay the groundwork for Villicana Winery—he and his wife, Monica, purchased 72 acres in the Adelaida hills. Alex and Monica chose the westside area for its calcium-rich limestone soil, which they believe "translates into rich, concentrated wines." With hands-on dedication to their new endeavor, the Villicanas personally planted each vine in their 15-acre vineyard.

Alex attends to all aspects of wine production, taking care of everything from farming the vines and the harvest of the grapes to crushing the fruit and making the wine. He and Monica also host the tasting bar on weekends. "Our plan is to remain a small winery, so we can put our efforts into continually increasing quality by producing impressive, limited lots of wine," Monica and Alex emphasize.

Villicana Winery's small-lot varietals have won numerous awards: Its 2001 Estate Merlot received the 2003 San Francisco International Wine Competition's Best of Show and double gold medal, and its 2000 Estate Cabernet Sauvignon won the gold medal at the 2003 Los Angeles County Fair.

Villicana Winery
2725 Adelaida Road
Paso Robles, CA 93446
(805) 239-9456
villicanawinery@earthlink.net
www.villicanawinery.com

Sub-AVA: Paso Robles

Owners:
Alex and Monica Villicana

Tasting Hours:
11 a.m. – 5 p.m. Saturday – Sunday
And by appointment most weekdays and holidays

Wines:
Zinfandel, Cabernet Sauvignon, Merlot, red wine blends

Winemaker's Specialty:
Cabernet Sauvignon

Winemaker: Alex Villicana

Flank Steak with Ginger-Peanut-Cabernet Sauce

2 lbs. flank steak
1/3 c. each soy sauce, honey, lime juice
1 tsp. onion powder
1/4 c. chicken broth
1/2 c. chunky peanut butter
1/2 c. Villicana Cabernet Sauvignon
2 Tbsp. each soy sauce and lime juice
2 tsp. honey
1 small ripe tomato, chopped
4 green onions, trimmed and minced
2 cloves garlic, minced
2 tsp. fresh ginger root, minced
1 jalapeño chili, seeded and minced
Skewers
White rice

Make marinade by mixing 1/3 cup soy sauce, honey, and lime juice with onion powder. Marinate meat for 24 hours. Put chicken broth, peanut butter, wine, 2 Tbsp. each soy sauce and lime juice, 2 tsp. honey, tomato, onions, garlic, ginger root, and chili in a large saucepan. Bring to a boil, reduce heat, and whisk while simmering for 2 minutes until thick and creamy. Grill meat, slice into long strips, and place on skewers. Place meat on a bed of white rice and drizzle with sauce. Serve with **Villicana Cabernet Sauvignon**.

WILD COYOTE ESTATE WINERY & VINEYARD

Wild Coyote Estate Winery & Vineyard's adobe-style tasting room is a blend of Mother Earth, Native American cultures, grapes, and wine. Owner and winemaker Gianni Manucci's eclectic Southwestern art collection and an authentic, life-size tepee make wine tasting at Wild Coyote a memorable experience.

Situated 1,800 feet above sea level seven miles west of Paso Robles, Wild Coyote evokes Gianni's long-standing interest in pueblo architecture and the culture of Native Americans. A former architect, Gianni has made numerous trips to the Southwest since the 1970s to study tribal customs, artwork, and building styles.

In 1995, Gianni changed careers, becoming a grape grower and winemaker like his grandfather. He purchased a 40-acre dry-orchard farm on Adelaida Road and two years later planted a vineyard with Syrah, Merlot, and Zinfandel grapes. The name "Wild Coyote" is a reference to the small pack of coyotes that roamed the property before the vineyard was planted.

Gianni designed and constructed the winery's Taos-style tasting room in 2002, using the numerous sketches and notes he'd made during his travels in New Mexico. "The tasting room was a challenge to construct and required many trips to Taos to bring back building materials I couldn't find on the Central Coast," Gianni admits. "I wanted to create an atmosphere where people could come and take up some of the energy and mysticism of Native American culture." In 2005, he built adjacent to the tasting room a five-bedroom, Casitas-style bed and breakfast.

Since its first releases, Wild Coyote has received critical acclaim. Its 1999 Syrah received a rating of 92 points from *Wine & Spirits* magazine, a gold medal at the 2001 San Francisco International Wine Competition, and a silver and a bronze at the 2001 Orange County Fair Wine Competition.

Although Gianni has enjoyed success as an architect and a winemaker, he claims he is "really an artist in spirit." A prolific stone sculptor, Gianni displays many of his pieces in the tasting-room gallery, including statuary depicting the Weeping Buddha, a bust of the Spiritual Chief, and, of course, a wild coyote.

Wild Coyote Estate Winery & Vineyard
3775 Adelaida Road
Paso Robles, CA 93446
(805) 610-1311
info@wildcoyote.biz
www.wildcoyote.biz

Sub-AVA: Paso Robles

Owner: Gianni Manucci

Tasting Hours:
11 a.m. – 5 p.m. daily

Wines: Zinfandel, Merlot, Syrah

Winemaker: Gianni Manucci

Wild Coyote Merlot-Braised Short Ribs

4 lbs. short ribs
Salt and pepper to taste
2 Tbsp. plus 1 tsp. *herbes de Provence*
4 Tbsp. olive oil
1 c. each shallots and onions, minced
1/2 c. each carrots and celery, finely chopped
3 Tbsp. minced garlic
2 c. each beef broth and Wild Coyote Merlot
3 medium tomatoes, diced
2 bay leaves
Fresh parsley and chives, chopped

Season ribs with salt, pepper, and 2 Tbsp. of the herbs. Heat oil in a heavy, ovenproof pot and brown ribs in batches, about 10 minutes per batch. Remove and keep warm. Pour off all but 3 Tbsp. fat from skillet and sauté shallots, onions, carrots, and celery for about 8 minutes until translucent. Add garlic and remaining herbs and sauté one minute more. Add broth and wine and bring to a boil. Add tomatoes and bay leaves. Return ribs to the pot, add water to barely cover the ribs, and bring to a boil. Cover and bake in a 350° oven for 2 to 2-1/2 hours until tender. Remove ribs, skim fat from liquid, and reduce sauce until "silky." Sprinkle ribs with parsley and chives and serve with sauce and **Wild Coyote Merlot.**

WILD HORSE WINERY & VINEYARDS

Located in historic Templeton, Wild Horse Winery & Vineyards takes its name from the wild mustangs that roam the plains east of its estate vineyard. These descendents of the first Spanish horses brought to California embody Wild Horse's "dynamic spirit and passionate dedication to winemaking."

Pioneer grape grower Ken Volk—one of the first vintners to recognize the Central Coast's world-class potential as a grape-growing region—established Wild Horse Winery & Vineyards in 1983. In 2003, Peak Wines International bought the winery but has continued Ken's Old World approach to winemaking. Peak Wines uses the sustainable viticulture practices initiated by Ken, including experimental programs in composting and the use of reclaimed water for irrigation and frost protection.

Wild Horse is one of the few wineries in the area that sources fruit from the entire Central Coast AVA. The winery purchases grapes from more than 40 vineyards within 16 sub-AVAs, showcasing the best characteristics the region has to offer. As a pioneer of Central Coast viticulture, Wild Horse believes that the most interesting wines result from working with a diversity of exceptional vineyards. Winemaker Mark Cummins emphasizes that

White Horse strives to embody regional character in each of its wines: "Wild Horse sources the 'right' sub-AVA for each particular varietal. I see the Central Coast AVA as a 'spice rack' of flavors for our blends."

Wild Horse Winery & Vineyards produces wines under two labels. The flagship "Wild Horse" label includes lead varietals Pinot Noir, Chardonnay, Merlot, and Cabernet Sauvignon, and three nationally distributed wines: Syrah, Viognier, and Zinfandel. The reserve label, "Cheval Sauvage"—French for "Wild Horse"—is limited to vintages deemed "exceptional" by the winemaking team. Wild Horse Winery & Vineyards also makes an array of "small-production," lesser-known varietals—Verdelho, Blaufrankisch, and Tempranillo, to name a few—which are sold exclusively at the tasting room.

Sidebar

Wild Horse Winery & Vineyards
1437 Wild Horse Winery Court
Templeton, CA 93465
(805) 434-2541
info@wildhorsewinery.com
www.wildhorsewinery.com

AVA: Central Coast

Owner: Peak Wines International

Tasting Hours:
11 a.m. – 5 p.m. daily

Wines: Pinot Noir, Merlot, Chardonnay, Cabernet Sauvignon, Viognier, Syrah Zinfandel

Winemaker's Specialty:
Pinot Noir

Winemaker: Mark Cummins

Duck with Pinot Noir Sauce

8 boneless duck breasts, rinsed and patted dry
1 bottle Wild Horse Pinot Noir
1/2 oz. dried porcini mushrooms
4 sprigs fresh thyme
2 cloves garlic
8 c. duck or rich chicken stock
Salt and freshly ground pepper to taste

In a heavy, non-reactive saucepan, combine wine, mushrooms, thyme, and garlic. Over high heat, reduce wine mixture to 1 cup. Add the stock and reduce by one-half. Remove sauce from heat, strain through a fine sieve, pressing hard on the mushrooms to extract all liquid. Return sauce to stove and reduce by one-half again. Remove from heat, skim any foam from surface, and keep warm. Season duck breasts with salt and pepper, place skin side down in sauté pan, and cook over medium-high heat about 7 minutes until golden brown and all fat has been rendered. Turn breasts, sear for 30 to 90 seconds, and remove from pan. Slice breasts into 1/4-inch slices, arrange in a fan-shaped pattern on warmed plates, and spoon wine-reduction sauce over all. Serve with rice pilaf and **Wild Horse Pinot Noir**.

WINDWARD VINEYARD

Windward Vineyard is situated on the windward side of Paso Robles, where cool Pacific Ocean breezes blow through the Templeton Gap. In true *monopole* French fashion—"monopole" means "exclusive possession"— owners Marc Goldberg and Maggie D'Ambrosia control all aspects of Windward's grape growing and winemaking. Using no other fruit but grapes from their own 15-acre vineyard, Marc and Maggie produce only one varietal, a Burgundian-style Pinot Noir.

It was their love for Pinot Noir that led Marc and Maggie to search the California coast for a vineyard site where they could grow the fragile varietal. In 1990, they purchased property on Paso Robles' west side because they believed "the area's cool climate and rocky, sloping, limestone-laden hillsides were hospitable for the production of stellar Pinot Noir." "Pinot Noir is the most difficult wine to make and the most reflective of the soil in which the grapes are grown," Marc emphasizes. "The vineyard speaks about itself through the wine. Our Pinot is unique because the conditions of the land and climate create it and therefore you can't get it anywhere else."

As the winemaker, Marc uses a cold maceration process and allows the juice to ferment in open-top containers. The Pinot is aged for approximately 14 months in French oak barrels made of staves that range from new to more than three years old. To retain flavor and structure, the wine is neither fined nor filtered.

The May 2004 *Pinot Report* awarded 92 points to Windward's Pinot Noir Paso Robles Monopole 2000, praising it as "very pretty and elegant in style . . . with a lot of unique regional character." In February 2004, *Santa Barbara News-Press* wine critic Dennis Schaefer wrote, "Windward's Pinots are perhaps among the most 'Burgundian' in California, their hallmark being their elegance and delicacy."

Marc and Maggie invite aficionados to savor their critically acclaimed Burgundian-style Pinot at Windward's tasting room or at the "Lath House," an inviting, outdoor picnic area surrounded by their estate vineyard.

Windward Vineyard
1380 Live Oak Road
Paso Robles, CA 93446
(805) 239-2565
info@windwardvineyard.com
www.windwardvineyard.com

Sub-AVA: Paso Robles

Owners:
Marc Goldberg,
Maggie D'Ambrosia

Tasting Hours:
11 a.m. – 5 p.m. daily

Wine: Pinot Noir

Winemaker: Marc Goldberg

Rustic Chicken Casserole

1 whole chicken, neck and giblets removed
Fresh sprigs of thyme, rosemary, and sage
40 cloves of garlic, unpeeled
Sea salt and freshly ground pepper to taste
1/2 c. Windward Vineyard Pinot Noir
1 c. flour
Enough water to make a paste

Place chicken, herbs, garlic, salt, pepper, and wine into a 3-quart casserole. Make a thick paste with the flour and water and roll into a "ribbon." Place the ribbon around the outside edge of casserole and press to make a seal. Bake at 350° for 1-1/2 hours. Break off bread seal and serve with the meal and the remaining **Windward Vineyard Pinot Noir**.

YORK MOUNTAIN WINERY

Tucked into the mountains midway between Cambria and Paso Robles, York Mountain Winery's weathered brick buildings look as if they've stood for more than a century. One of the oldest, continuously operating wineries in San Luis Obispo County, York Mountain's beginnings date back to 1882, when Andrew York purchased an apple orchard with a small plot of wine grapes and founded Ascension Winery, as York Mountain was first known.

With the help of his sons and grandsons, Andrew expanded the vineyard and planted Mission, Zinfandel, and Alicante Bouschet grapes. The York family tended the vineyard, crushed the fruit, and made wine that was sold locally and also shipped in barrels via horse-drawn wagon to the San Joaquin Valley, and to the coast for delivery by steamship to San Francisco.

Following Prohibition, Andrew's sons, who by then owned the winery, continued to make wine and expanded their plantings. About the same time, Polish statesman and pianist Ignace Paderewski began bringing Zinfandel grapes from his Adelaida vineyard to York Mountain to be made into wine.

In the 1970s, winemaker Max Goldman purchased the nearly 100-year-old winery from the York family and continued the York winemaking tradition for more than three decades. Max sold the historic winery in 2001 to David and Mary Weyrich, the owners of Martin & Weyrich Winery & Tasting Room in Paso Robles, making them the third family to own the landmark property.

Today, York Mountain Winery is located in one of the smallest recognized American viticulture areas, the York Mountain sub-AVA. The old winery still produces Zinfandel but has added to its portfolio Pinot Noir, Chardonnay, Black Muscat, Merlot, Viognier, Roussanne, Cabernet Sauvignon, Zinfandel, and Syrah.

Combining respect for the venerable winery's heritage with their own knowledge of the local wine industry, the Weyrich family is dedicated to the preservation of this operating historic landmark.

York Mountain Winery
7505 York Mountain Road West
Paso Robles, CA 93465
(805) 238-3925
sales@yorkmountainwinery.com
www.yorkmountainwinery.com

Sub-AVA: York Mountain

Owners: David and Mary Weyrich

Tasting Hours:
10 a.m. – 4 p.m. daily (Summer)
10 a.m. – 4 p.m. Wed. – Sun. (Winter)

Wines: Pinot Noir, Chardonnay, Black Muscat, Merlot, Viognier, Roussanne, Cabernet Sauvignon, Zinfandel, Syrah

Winemakers' Specialty: Pinot Noir

Winemakers:
Craig Reed, Alan Kinne

Beet Salad with Walnuts and Gorgonzola

8 small beets
1-1/2 tsp. coarse sea salt, divided
1/3 c. olive oil
1 tsp. Dijon mustard
1 Tbsp. plus 1 tsp. rice vinegar
2 Tbsp. green onions, sliced
1/2 tsp. pepper, freshly ground
1 clove garlic, bruised lightly with
   flat part of a knife
4 c. baby salad greens
1/2 c. toasted walnuts, chopped
3 oz. Gorgonzola cheese, crumbled
Fresh parsley, chopped, to taste

Bring 4 cups water and 1 tsp. salt to a boil. Add beets and cook about 20 minutes until tender. Drain beets and cool. Peel and cut into 1-inch pieces and set aside. In a small bowl, mix oil, mustard, vinegar, onions, pepper, garlic, and remaining 1/2 tsp. salt. Stir for 1 to 2 minutes to impart garlic taste. Add beets, cover, and refrigerate several hours or overnight. Remove garlic clove. In a large bowl, place greens, walnuts, cheese, and parsley. Remove beets with a slotted spoon and add to greens. Whisk olive oil mixture to blend and pour over salad. Toss. Serve with **York Mountain Pinot Noir**.

ZENAIDA CELLARS

In 1758, Carl Linnaeus gave the mourning dove its Latin, scientific classification, *Zenaida macroura*, because he found the dove a beautiful creature like his wife, Zenaida. Zenaida Cellars owner Eric Ogorsolka has always liked the story of Linnaeus and the dove and thought "Zenaida" would make a memorable name for his own "memorable wines."

Latin has been a part of Eric's background since he earned a bachelor's degree in biology at California Polytechnic State University in San Luis Obispo. After graduation, Eric took a roundabout path to winemaking, exploring numerous career options and for a time working as a fisheries biologist for the state of California.

In 1994, Eric began making small lots of "experimental wines" with grapes from his family's 65-acre estate vineyard, which is located on historic property west of Highway 101 in Paso Robles. Four years later, Eric built a rustic, mission-style winery with 16-foot cellar doors on the 100-year-old homestead site and launched the Zenaida Cellars wine label.

Zenaida's vines grow in lean soil layered with calcareous shale, limestone, clay, and sand. Vines are vertically trellised, which allows for maximum sunlight and airflow. Eric explains that the growing technique "maximizes the

leaf-surface area, allowing good sugar production and even ripening of the fruit," and believes that "the varied soils in the west Paso Robles region are the key to complexity in our wines."

Wine Enthusiast's November 2001 issue, "Super Wine Values Discovered," gave 91 points to Zenaida's 1999 Syrah. A 2003 issue of *Vine Times* magazine declared Eric's 2001 Estate Zinfandel to be "a well-balanced bomb!"

Overnight visitors can enjoy a comfortable and peaceful retreat in "The Loft," located above the Zenaida Cellars tasting room. The 1,500-square-foot, two-bedroom guest suite has a private, covered deck that overlooks the estate vineyards.

Zenaida Cellars
1550 Highway 46 West
Paso Robles, CA 93446
(805) 227-0382
info@zenaidacellars.com
www.zenaidacellars.com

Sub-AVA: Paso Robles

Owner: Eric Ogorsolka

Tasting Hours:
11 a.m. – 5 p.m. daily

Wines: Zinfandel, Syrah, Cabernet Sauvignon, Chardonnay, Viognier, Zephyr Rhône-style blend

Winemaker's Specialties: Zinfandel, Syrah, estate blends

Winemaker: Eric Ogorsolka

Dijon-Dill Pork Chops

6 1-inch-thick pork chops
3 to 4 Tbsp. Dijon mustard
2 Tbsp. unsalted butter
1 large onion, thinly sliced
3 Tbsp. flour
1-1/2 c. chicken stock
3/4 c. heavy cream
1/2 tsp. each salt and white pepper
1 tsp. fresh dill, chopped

Pound chops with a mallet and brush generously with mustard. In a large, heavy skillet, melt butter and brown chops. Remove chops from pan and set aside. Add onion to pan and cook over medium heat until golden brown, about 5 minutes. Remove skillet from direct heat and add flour, stirring well to combine. Return skillet to heat, add broth, and bring to a boil, stirring constantly. Add cream, salt, pepper, dill, and chops to skillet. Cover, reduce heat and simmer for 50 to 60 minutes or until tender, turning once during cooking. Serve chops with sauce and **Zenaida Cellars Zinfandel**.

GLOSSARY OF WINE TERMS

American oak barrels   Barrels made from oak wood of the species *quercus alba*, from a U.S. forest

Appellation   A name used to designate the official geographic origin of a wine

Balance   The interrelationship of a wine's alcohol, tannin, residual sugar, and acid content

Battonage   The process of stirring wine as it ages on its lees in the barrel

Blend   A wine that is made from two or more lots of wine, usually from the juice of two or more grape varieties

Body   The perceived "weight" or viscosity of a wine in the mouth

Bouquet   The fragrance of a wine, which includes several aromatic elements formed by the oxidation of fruit acids and alcohol

Calcareous   Of, like, or containing calcium carbonate, calcium, or lime

Character   A tasting term used to describe the flavor elements of a wine that give it substance or integrity

Clone   A sub-variety of a grape variety comprising a group of genetically identical vines propagated asexually from a single vine

Cold soak   A pre-fermentation maceration process where crushed grapes are stored at a low temperature to enhance the color of the juice

Dry   The opposite of the term "sweet" when describing wine

Estate wines   Wines that are produced from grapes owned or controlled by the winery

Fermentation   The gradual, natural process that occurs when yeast transforms the sugar in grape juice into alcohol

Fining   To refine or clarify wine

Finish   The taste of the wine that remains in the mouth after it has been swallowed

French oak barrels   Barrels made from oak wood of the species *quercus robur*, from the forests of France, considered the finest type of oak for aging most white wines

Fruit forward   Having the first impression of flavors and aromas suggestive of fruit

Horizontal wine tasting   A side-by-side wine tasting of the same wine varieties

Lees   The natural sediment of grape skins, pulp, and yeast that settle to the bottom of the barrel or vat as a wine ferments and ages. Wines undergo raking to remove these sediments.

Maceration   The contact of the grape skins with the juice to leach the skin's color, tannin, and other substances into the juice

New oak   Oak barrels that are brand-new or that have been used four or fewer times

New World   A collective term applied to wine-making countries located outside Europe

Old oak/neutral oak   Oak barrels at least five years old that have lost most of their oaky character

Old vine   A term for a vine whose fruit is deemed exceptional due to the vine being, generally, at least 40 years old and producing a low-yield crop

Old World   A collective term for the wine-making countries of Europe

Phylloxera   A parasite that attacks the roots of grapevines, causing the death of the plant

Pomace   The pulp of grape-skin and grape-seed residue

Punching down   Breaking up grape-skin caps and other solids during red-wine fermentation

Raking   Moving wine from one barrel to another in order to separate it from settled solids—the lees—at the bottom.

Regulated deficit irrigation (RDI)   An irrigation-management technique that limits water to stress vines, reducing fruit quantity and thereby increasing fruit quality

Reserve   A wine deemed finer than the normal version of the same wine

Rootstock   A root in which a graft is inserted for propagating plants. Specific rootstocks are chosen for disease and pest resistance as well as for soil conditions.

Single-vineyard wine   A wine made from the grapes of one vineyard that usually displays the name of the vineyard on its label

Structure   The interaction of a wine's alcohol, acid, tannin, and sugar components, which contribute to its texture and feel in the mouth

Sur lie   A wine that has aged on its lees in the barrel

Tannin   A flavor component derived from grape seeds, stems, and skins. Oak barrels also contain tannin.

Terroir   A French term used to describe the growing conditions in a vineyard, including soil, drainage, exposure, climate, microclimate, and other factors that make a site unique

Transverse valley   A valley lying on an east/west axis, with one end opening to the ocean

Varietal   A wine named for the grape variety from which it was made

Varietal character   The characteristics of a specific grape variety

Vertical wine tasting   A side-by-side wine tasting of wines of the same variety from the same winery that are sequenced by vintage

Vinification   The process of making wine

Vintage   The year in which a wine's grapes grew and were harvested

Viticulture   The process of growing grapes

Yeasts   One-celled microorganisms that grow quickly in a liquid containing sugar, responsible for transforming grape juice into wine

RECIPE INDEX

WHERE TO STAY

The author provides the following list of accommodations for the convenience of visitors to the Central Coast's wine country. The listing does not constitute an endorsement of any particular establishment. Guests are encouraged to visit the Web sites or contact the proprietors before making reservations.

THE SAN LUIS OBISPO AREA

Apple Farm Inn
2015 Monterey Street
San Luis Obispo, CA 93401
(805) 544-2040
(800) 374-3705 toll free
www.applefarm.com

Bridge Creek Inn
5300 Righetti Road
San Luis Obispo, CA 93401
(805) 544-3003
www.bridgecreekinn.com

The Cliffs at Shell Beach
2757 Shell Beach Road
Shell Beach, CA 93449
(805) 773-5000
(800) 826-7827 toll free
www.cliffsresort.com

Embassy Suites Hotel San Luis Obispo
333 Madonna Road
San Luis Obispo, CA 93405
(805) 549-0800
(800) 362-2779 toll free
www.embassysuites.com

Garden Street Inn
1212 Garden Street
San Luis Obispo, CA 93401
(805) 545-9802
www.gardenstreetinn.com

Heritage Inn
978 Olive Street
San Luis Obispo, CA 93405
(805) 544-7440
www.heritageinnslo.com

Madonna Inn
100 Madonna Road
San Luis Obispo, CA 93405
(805) 543-3000
(800) 543-9666 toll free
www.madonnainn.com

Petit Soleil
1473 Monterey Street
San Luis Obispo CA 93401
(805) 549-0321
(800) 676-1588 toll free
www.petitsoleilslo.com

Suite Edna B & B
1653 Old Price Canyon Road
San Luis Obispo, CA 93401
(805) 544-8062
www.oldedna.com

THE PASO ROBLES AREA

Almond Hill Vineyard Bed & Breakfast
1760 Valley Quail Place
Paso Robles, CA 93446
(805) 239-7898
www.hometown.aol.com/almondhillvinyrd

Carlton Hotel
6005 El Camino Real
Atascadero, CA 93422
(805) 461-5100
(877) 204-9830 toll free
www.the-carlton.com

Carriage Vineyards Bed & Breakfast
4337 South El Pomar
Templeton, CA 93465
(805) 227-6807
(800) 617-7911 toll free
www.carriagevineyards.com

Chanticleer Vineyard Bed & Breakfast
(805) 226-0600
www.chanticleervineyardbb.com

Creekside Bed & Breakfast
5325 Vineyard Drive
Paso Robles, CA 93446
(805) 227-6585
www.thecreeksidebb.com

Dunning Vineyards Country Inn
1953 Niderer Road
Paso Robles, CA 93446
(805) 238-4763
www.dunningvineyards.com

JUST Inn
11680 Chimney Rock Road
Paso Robles, CA 93446
(805) 237-4149
www.justinwine.com

The Loft at Zenaida Cellars
1550 Highway 46 West
Paso Robles, CA 93446
(805) 227-0382
(800) ZEN-LOFT toll free
www.zenaidacellars.com

Orchard Hill Farm
5415 Vineyard Drive
Paso Robles, CA 93446
(805) 239-9680
www.orchardhillbb.com

Summerwood Inn
2175 Arbor Road
Paso Robles, CA 93446
(805) 227-1111
www.summerwoodwine.com

Tobin James Cellars Bed & Breakfast
8950 Union Road
Paso Robles, CA 93446
(805) 239-2204
www.tobinjames.com

Villa Toscana Bed & Breakfast
4230 Buena Vista Drive
Paso Robles, CA
(805) 238-5600
www.martinweyrich.com

Vineyard Cottage Inn
7840 Vineyard Drive
Paso Robles, CA 93446
(805) 239-4678
www.wineriesofpasorobles.com

The Vineyard House
3380 Branch Road
Paso Robles, CA 93446
(805) 226-9922 X23
www.bianchiwine.com

Wild Coyote Estate Winery &
Vineyard Bed & Breakfast
3775 Adelaida Road
Paso Robles, CA 93446
(805) 610-1311
www.wildcoyote.biz

RAIL TOURS

For transportation, accommodations and tour packages to San Luis Obispo wineries, contact:

The Overland Trail
1949 Club Lounge Railway Car
2054 South Halladay Street
Santa Ana, CA 92707
(714) 546-6923
(800) 539-7245 toll free
www.overlandtrail.com

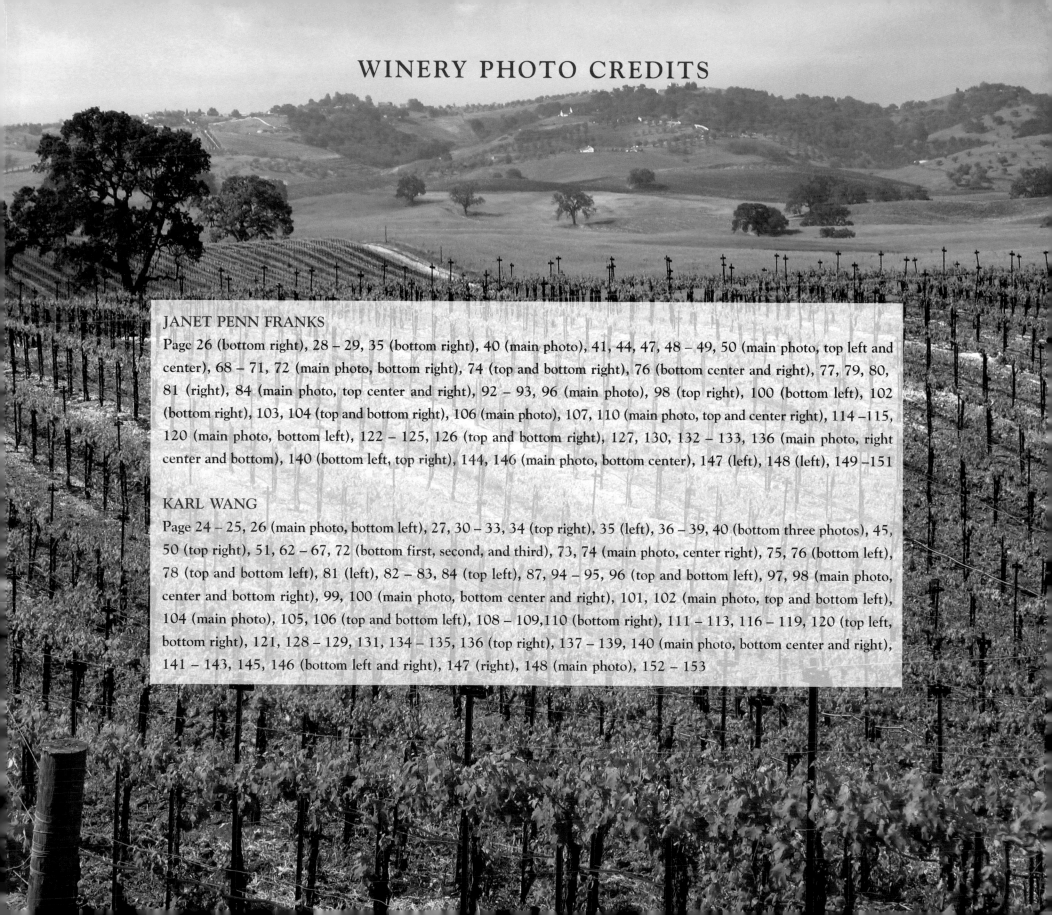

WINERY PHOTO CREDITS

JANET PENN FRANKS

Page 26 (bottom right), 28 – 29, 35 (bottom right), 40 (main photo), 41, 44, 47, 48 – 49, 50 (main photo, top left and center), 68 – 71, 72 (main photo, bottom right), 74 (top and bottom right), 76 (bottom center and right), 77, 79, 80, 81 (right), 84 (main photo, top center and right), 92 – 93, 96 (main photo), 98 (top right), 100 (bottom left), 102 (bottom right), 103, 104 (top and bottom right), 106 (main photo), 107, 110 (main photo, top and center right), 114 –115, 120 (main photo, bottom left), 122 – 125, 126 (top and bottom right), 127, 130, 132 – 133, 136 (main photo, right center and bottom), 140 (bottom left, top right), 144, 146 (main photo, bottom center), 147 (left), 148 (left), 149 –151

KARL WANG

Page 24 – 25, 26 (main photo, bottom left), 27, 30 – 33, 34 (top right), 35 (left), 36 – 39, 40 (bottom three photos), 45, 50 (top right), 51, 62 – 67, 72 (bottom first, second, and third), 73, 74 (main photo, center right), 75, 76 (bottom left), 78 (top and bottom left), 81 (left), 82 – 83, 84 (top left), 87, 94 – 95, 96 (top and bottom left), 97, 98 (main photo, center and bottom right), 99, 100 (main photo, bottom center and right), 101, 102 (main photo, top and bottom left), 104 (main photo), 105, 106 (top and bottom left), 108 – 109,110 (bottom right), 111 – 113, 116 – 119, 120 (top left, bottom right), 121, 128 – 129, 131, 134 – 135, 136 (top right), 137 – 139, 140 (main photo, bottom center and right), 141 – 143, 145, 146 (bottom left and right), 147 (right), 148 (main photo), 152 – 153

REFERENCES

Research materials used in the preparation of this book include the following:

Books and reports

· *Aged in Oak: The Story of the Santa Barbara Wine Industry* (UCSB Graduate Program in Public Historical Studies/Santa Barbara County Vintners' Association, 1998)

· *California Wine Winners 2004*, edited by J.T. Devine

· *Central Coast Wine Tour from San Francisco to Santa Barbara*, by Richard Paul Hinkle (1977)

· *A Companion to California Wine: An Encyclopedia of Wine and Winemaking from the Mission Period to the Present*, by Charles Sullivan (1998)

· *Crop Statistics for 2004* (San Luis Obispo County Department of Agriculture and Weights and Measures, 2005)

· *Great Wine Made Simple*, by Andrea Immer (2000)

· *History of Winemaking in San Luis Obispo County Research Report* (San Luis Obispo Historical Society, 2004)

· *Looking Back Into the Middle Kingdom, San Luis Obispo*, by Daniel E. Krieger (1988)

· *New California Wine*, by Matt Kramer (2004)

· *Vineyards on the Mission Trail: The Wineland of Santa Barbara and San Luis Obispo Counties*, by Larry Roberts and Carol Manning (California Central Coast Wine Growers Association, 1981)

· *Vino de California*, by Daniel E. Krieger (May 10, 2003)

· *World Book Encyclopedia* (World Book Inc., 1990)

Newspaper articles

· "City and County News: Hasbrouck's Ranch" (*San Luis Obispo Tribune*, March 30, 1883)

· "Louis Dallidet's Diary Captures Daily Life on a San Luis Obispo Vineyard," by Daniel E. Krieger (*Telegram-Tribune*, July 27, 1985)

· "Our Wines" (*Daily Republic*, Jan. 29, 1887)

· St. Remy Vineyard ad (*Arroyo Grande Herald*, Dec. 19, 1896)

· "Three Generations of York Family Have Owned Winery" (*Telegram-Tribune*, Aug. 7, 1957)

· "Trip Around County: Some Notes on the Wine Industry" (*Morning Tribune*, Oct. 6, 1907)

· "The Wine Industry" (*Morning Tribune*, Nov. 8, 1907)

· "Winemaking" (*The Daily Republic*, Oct. 3, 1889)

Web sites

· *www.cellarnotes.net*

· *www.pasowine.com*

· *www.slowine.com*

· *www.thevinetimes.com*

· *www.wineandspiritsmagazine.com*

· *www.wineanswers.com*

· *www.wineinstitute.org*

· *www.winespectator.com*

· and individual Web sites from all featured wineries